THE
COROMANDEL

For Dinah and Maria
companions in travel

THE COROMANDEL

First published in 1993 by
TANDEM PRESS
2 Rugby Road, Birkenhead, Auckland 10
New Zealand

Copyright © 1993 text: Michael King
Copyright © 1993 photographs: Robin Morrison

ISBN 0 908884 29 X

Design and production by Moscow Design
Typesetting by Typocrafters Ltd
Printed in Hong Kong by Everbest Printing Co.

THE
COROMANDEL

Text: Michael King

Photographs: Robin Morrison

TANDEM PRESS

CONTENTS

Curier Island

Great Barrier Island

Cape Colville
Port Jackson
Fletcher Bay
Stony Bay
Port Charles
Waikawau
Waiaro
Colville Bay
Te Moehau
Parfu
Te Whau Point
Happy Jack Island
Motukawao Group
Whangamui Island
HAURAKI GULF

Red Mercury Island
Great Mercury Island

Tuateawa
Kennedy Bay
Whanagapoua
COROMANDEL
Te Kouma
Manaia

Opito
Kuaotunu
Tahanga

Mercury Bay

Castle Rock
WHITIANGA
Cooks Beach
Hahei

Hot Water Beach

Whenuakite

Coroglen
(Gum Town)

Tapu
Waiomu
Te Puru
Tararu
THAMES
Kopu

Table Mountain

FIRTH OF THAMES

The Aldermen

Slipper Island

Wharekawa Harbour
Paku   Shoe Island
Pauanui
Tairua   Onui
Tairua River
Opoutere
Onemana
WHANGAMATA
Hikuai

Waihou   River

Waihi Beach

Whiritoa
Mataora

Hikutaia

Paeroa
Mackaytown
Karangahake
Mt Te Aroha

Waitekauri
WAIHI
Waikino

FOREWORD

Although it is joined to New Zealand at the armpit of the Hauraki Plains, the Coromandel Peninsula is in many respects — cultural and geographical — like an island. It is made up for the most part of a series of small communities bordered by water and high mountains. It has an appearance, a history and a lifestyle that set it apart from the rest of the country and contribute to what can only be regarded as a distinctive New Zealand subculture.

This book is an exploration of the ingredients of that subculture. It is also an explanation of how things came to be the way they are on the Coromandel and a depiction of being there. We hope it will have resonance for those who already know the peninsula; and that it will serve as an introduction for those who do not.

Everybody we approached for help with this project responded with enthusiasm: the residents whose features and home places appear here, and those who provided information and advice. We thank them all.

Michael King
Robin Morrison

Riding the range on the 309 road, in view of Castle Rock.

CHAPTER ONE

THE COROMANDEL: A PERSONAL ENCOUNTER

The shadowy tents beneath the pines
The surfboards and the fishing-lines
Tell that our life might be
One of simplicity . . .

So children burn the seastained wood
And tell the present as a good
Knowing that bonfires are
Important as a star.

M K Joseph,
Mercury Bay Eclogue

The Coromandel Peninsula loomed large in the lore of our family. One of my sisters was conceived there when my parents were trapped by bad weather in a tent at Port Charles. A family friend from childhood days retired there, making extravagant boasts about the regenerative powers of the region's climate (30 years later I found him there still, in a rest home, celebrating his 97th birthday and boasting that the only thing he'd had to give up was sex). Later, towards the end of the 1950s, we went there on our first major holiday away from home.

Every detail of that camping expedition has stayed with me, because what we saw that summer was so different from anything that I, brought up in the lower North Island, had seen before. We travelled in a Wolseley 444, hauling a trailer piled with tent, bedding and blackened cooking utensils. We circumnavigated the peninsula from east to west.

It was more like visiting an island than another part of New Zealand. The roads were unsealed and we threw up a tail of dust. We made camp between rocky promontories where we found a series of perfect bays, each with its own river or lagoon, each with a crescent of white sand. The mountain range of the interior seemed as high as the Himalayas, but cloaked in rain forest rather than snow. Nikau palms added to the island ambiance. And the people we visited grew exotic plants we had never seen before: hibiscus, pawpaw, bananas, even tea.

Casually, we came across unadvertised wonders: groves of kauri as silent and as high as cathedrals; high waterfalls dropping into deep pools surrounded by ferns; decaying wooden dams from the days of kauri logging; derelict mines like ruined abbeys; shafts driven vertically and horizontally into rock; shorelines littered with petrified wood and gemstones; fossils in creek beds; contours of fortified pa on almost every seaside headland. I found quartz crystals, opalised jasper and kauri gum, and a moa bone fish hook on the surface of a crumbling beach midden.

We camped first by the estuary at Whangamata. The settlement was no more than a cluster of fibrolite baches behind the dunes. We romped in the surf and at low tide scooped out feeds of tuatua.

Camping on the beach at Mercury Bay near Whitianga.

Further north we climbed Paku headland at Tairua, the most precipitous pa site on the peninsula, and looked down on a pine-covered sandspit called Pauanui. In the sand at Hot Water Beach we dug our own thermal pools and regulated the temperature through ditches of advancing seawater.

We saw few people other than fellow campers. We were never jostled. Whitianga was the largest settlement on the east coast, but even that had the character and dimensions of a fishing village. There, hanging from a gibbet on the wharf, we saw our first marlin, a vanquished giant. We went over the range to Coromandel township, whose shop fronts looked like a set for a Hollywood western. Then we tracked north and east again, over the hill to our major destination.

Kennedy's Bay confirmed the impression of the peninsula as an outpost of Island Polynesia. There were more palms and abundant tree ferns. A small community of Ngati Porou supplied us with fish and fresh vegetables. We snorkelled in clear water off the rocks and found bountiful colonies of paua, kina and crayfish. We slept in a farmer's barn behind a beach so bleached it resembled ground coral. We lit fires in the evening for cooking and for talking around late into the flickering night. Sometimes we dragged our sleeping bags outside, under the wheeling galaxy, and identified constellations and spotted shooting stars until we fell into sleep.

Around the northern corner of the bay,

Sarah Bell in her garden at Tuateawa.

Two decades on; Sarah Bell's former home, still surrounded by pohutukawa, puriri and palms.

at Tuateawa, we found Sarah Bell, Maori widow of a dentist, living in what seemed to me the most perfect house I had seen. A cluster of cloned cottages, it nestled high in a nikau and puriri grove overlooking the coast. Rooms had been added when needed, like cells in a beehive. The garden bloomed with cacti, flowers and fruit. The paths were lined with shells. Inside, Mrs Bell gave us a spectacular afternoon tea of woodstove scones and showed us her husband's collection of Maori artifacts. We left with a loaf of home-baked bread and a warm recollection of Coromandel hospitality.

Eventually, reluctantly — for the sun shone still and the pace of life was slow — we headed for home down the west coast. Here we saw old homesteads in narrowing valleys and rata blooming scarlet in the bush; then a long strip of rocks and shingle beaches overhung with crimson pohutukawas and dotted with baches made from recently discarded trams. Thames, our final destination on the peninsula, still retained much of its character as a gold mining town in the remains of stamper batteries, Victorian pubs and the miners' cottages around the outskirts. Our last taste of Coromandel was a meal of flounder, fresh caught from the Firth. Then it was home to work, school and suburbia.

Hotwater Beach: baths in the sand scooped out by hand.

Waiomu on the west side of the peninsula.

A decade passed before I went back to the Coromandel. But the shapes of its hills and coast remained encoded on my mind. And I carried my rocks and artifacts about with me like a reliquary. I knew I would return. There was so much there that pulled and pleased and interested me.

My first return involved a degree of disappointment, however. By the late 1960s the peninsula was no longer a sleepy island. It was becoming a target for developments generated by the growth of Auckland and Hamilton and the expansion of their commercial activities. I spent my honeymoon at Whangamata, which had grown thoughtlessly ugly and ungainly. Further north, plans were in motion for urban-style subdivisions on Paku headland and at Pauanui. Hot Water Beach, Hahei, Cook's Beach in Mercury Bay and Whangapoua were all scheduled for 'development'. So was Whiritoa. The peninsula was still beautiful, stunningly so in places, and this was the focal point for promoting and selling the subdivision schemes. But it was no longer a base purely for the kinds of low-impact camping and baching that we had witnessed and shared 10 years before.

I had joined the staff of a Hamilton newspaper which gave extensive coverage to analysis of the policies then favoured by the two major local bodies on the peninsula. People supporting development stressed the gains to be made from making the peninsula accessible to and comfortable for a larger population. They drew

Main street, Coromandel, in the 'fifties.

Coromandel township: shopfronts like a set from a Western movie.

attention to the need to create employment in the region. They also emphasised the rights of private property owners to dispose of their land in whatever ways they regarded as most appropriate or most profitable.

The conservationists, largely those who had spent their summers camping and tramping and boating around the peninsula, argued for the need to retain the 'character and integrity' of the region, to preserve habitats for the benefit of wildlife, and to protect historic sites for posterity. They also advocated leaving the coastline accessible for the recreation and enjoyment of as wide a range of people as possible.

Neither side 'won' the argument. But the development lobby was most influential with the makers of public policy. I witnessed the bulldozing of a Maori pa site at Whiritoa and watched onlookers scramble to collect artifacts scattered by the blade. I also reported the views of an ecologist

Saving Coromandel kauri in the Manaia block.

who described plans for the Pauanui subdivision as an example of 'bringing Pakuranga to the beach'.

Sections of native bush which had survived the slash-and-burn policies of the logging and mining eras were also under threat at this time. The New Zealand Forest Service was pursuing a policy they called 'sustainable yield', which gave them the right to fell the surviving giants of the forest. Acting on 'information received', I tramped into the Manaia Block on the eastern side of the peninsula with the Hamon brothers and a Colville farmer named Neville Evans. There we found over 300 large kauris, the tallest of them marked for felling. Tracks on which they were to be hauled out had already been bulldozed to the bases of the trunks. The damage was appalling.

Armed with this information we persuaded the Minister of Forests to come to the Coromandel to see for himself the effects of 'sustainable yield'. He did so, and the result was a government decision to set aside the whole area as a forest sanctuary in 1972. Throughout the rest of the decade the remaining areas of virgin bush were also reserved, as forest parks or Crown land, and saved from the millers' saws.

In 1969 I was asked to cover the Cook Bicentenary celebrations in Mercury Bay. There, on the beach where James Cook and his men observed the transit of the planet Mercury across the face of the sun in November 1769 and took possession of the surrounding countryside in the name

Looking through a miniature forest of aloes towards
Happy Jack Island off the west coast south of Colville.

of King George III, I heard gentle and implicit criticism of policies that seemed at that time destined to shape the peninsula's future appearance and economic growth.

The keynote speaker, the great Cook scholar J C Beaglehole, who had just been appointed to the Order of Merit, described how he and his wife had taken a summer holiday on the Coromandel between 30 and 40 years earlier. They had tramped around the coast from Kennedy's Bay to Whitianga, and then on to Cook's Beach beside the Purangi River. There they spent the night on the verandah of an empty bach.

'Next morning was absolutely crystalline,' Beaglehole told his audience, 'the sea and the sand as pure as the air and the early sun; and I walked along the beach by the side of the sea, round that magnificent curve, up to the edge of what James Cook called Oyster River. On the other side of the stream two or three Maori figures appeared and looked at me: otherwise the whole bay, from sea to the hills, was empty and silent. And yet I felt something. It was nothing to do with a half-stirring breeze, or the gradually warming sun, though it was a sort of faint tingling of the mind.

'It was an experience I have had only twice at other times: once crossing Botany Bay, also on a clear calm morning, the other on a blazing hot day on a beach below casuarina trees on Tahiti. I don't want to use that old expression "the trembling of a veil", but it was like that. And on the other side, just beyond my vision, was a ship, and a boat rowing towards the shore; and somewhere or other, just floating beyond the reach of my ear, was the sound of words. I almost, before I turned back, caught sight of the *Endeavour*, I almost heard the words of eighteenth-century sailors . . .

'My idea of a memorial to Cook,' Beaglehole concluded, 'is a place left as nearly as possible as he found it — so that you can, when conditions are favourable, almost feel his presence. I am not, altogether, in favour of progress, development, of more and more people living in more and more houses — even if the people and houses are undeniably nice. There is something very satisfactory about a waste of sandhills.'

14

*Mataora Bay: home of the last
traditional tattooist and thriving
Ngati Porou community up to
the 1940s.*

The psychic residue of which Beaglehole spoke, the awareness of the ethos of previous human activity and emotion, is strong on the Coromandel; or at least on those parts of the peninsula which have not been sealed off in concrete and asphalt. I myself felt it most strongly the following year when the Ngati Porou elder Te Kani Poata took me down to the coast at Mataora Bay.

Generations before, Mataora had been named after the demi-god who brought tattooing to human-kind from the Underworld. In one of those extraordinary coincidences so often associated with Maori life, the last tohunga who did tattooing in the traditional manner, Te Kani's father Tame Poata, had died at the bay in 1942. We went back there to visit his grave and to view the relics of the community that had lived there until just after the Second World War.

In the cemetery, high above Mataora Bay.

Like Kennedy's Bay, Mataora had been given to Ngati Porou by the Hauraki tribes, largely as a way station for the coastal vessels that sailed between the East Coast and Auckland in the nineteenth century. It was a perfect and characteristic Coromandel Bay: a headland to the north, a white sand beach, a lagoon and river mouth to the south, and then another headland with a tiny island off the point. Ngati Porou had built their settlement in the valley flat behind the beach. Their cemetery was on the clifftop south of the southern arm of the bay.

By 1970 the only buildings standing

intact were the schoolroom and the teacher's house, both built of heart kauri at the turn of the century. A couple of smaller houses survived, but open to the weather. Only arum lilies and old roses marked the sites of others. Close to the beach was a collapsed meeting house. As we walked among these ruins, Te Kani spoke of his early life there: who had lived in which house, where the vegetable gardens were, the routines for fishing off the beach, where in the bush behind they had taken pigeon and kiwi for the pot. He also pointed out an enormous pohutukawa halfway along the beach which covered the burial site of an earlier people. 'There's taonga there. And bones,' he said. 'And if anyone touched them they drowned. Or suffered some other catastrophe.'

At last we climbed the path to the southern cliff and the urupa. The headstones stood among manuka, bracken and rewarewa, high above the sea, facing east according to the oldest of Polynesian burial customs. 'Here's Dad,' he said. 'And his needles and chisels. We buried them with him in a silver box. They were too sacred for anybody else to touch. They'd drawn blood from the most tapu women in nearly every tribe.'

So here had ended one of the most ancient of Maori practices. Here, too, a community had died. 'We all moved into Waihi, so that the men could work in the mine,' said Te Kani. 'And when that closed in the early 1950s, a lot of them went on to Auckland. But they have their beginnings here, those families. This is their turangawaewae. Everything that's good and bad about them comes from this place.'

And, indeed, some of the names on the headstones were known to me: people whose descendants had gone on to successful careers in Te Ao Hou, the new Maori urban world. Some were not familiar to me then but would become so. Like the Tamihere family, one of whose sons, David Wayne, spent time brooding on tribal land at Mataora in 1989 before he went north to meet two Swedish tourists near Thames.

17

After I moved from Waikato to Wellington in the early 1970s, I lost touch with the Coromandel for another decade. When I shifted north again in the early 1980s I returned to the peninsula with the intention of finding a home there. Impressions cast in childhood are pervasive and persuasive; deep within me I retained the imprint of mountains, estuaries and coastlines. In spite of what I had regarded previously as the intrusions and blemishes of large-scale subdivision, the new communities were beginning to look established, starting to seem as if they belonged where they stood. And they housed a whole new generation of Coromandel residents and holiday-makers, boaties, trampers, campers, many of whom shared the conservation ethic evolved among the descendants of earlier settlers.

Besides, whole tracts of the peninsula were unspoiled still. It remained possible to replenish the spirit in virgin bush. The silhouette of the ranges was unchanged and juxtaposed spectacularly with the coastline. Kilometres of beachfront were uninhabited. The gemstones, the petrified wood, the fossils, the gum — all still littered the less accessible creek beds and shoreline. Most of the Maori sites were undisturbed. A recently merged district council and a new generation of local body members seemed more inclined to protect these features than had their predecessors.

I re-established my relationship with the region and its inhabitants by taking my second wife on a circumnavigation of the peninsula that matched the one we had made as a family a quarter of a century before. I looked too for old friends, some of whom (like Mrs Bell at Tuateawa) had died. Others, like Curly Hale at Kennedy's Bay (who had survived 28 days at sea when his fishing boat was blown offshore), and Florence Harsant at Hahei, were still triumphantly and ebulliently alive.

Florence and her husband Horace had accomplished the full New Zealand pioneer experience in their parallel lifetimes. He had gone with his brother at the turn of the century to Coroglen to open a store after both had spent time in the bush as axemen. From the profits of trading they had been able to buy most of the coastal land between Mercury Bay and Hahei. Then they broke it in for farming.

Florence joined him immediately after the First World War, following an astonishing career of her

Florence Harsant, surviving pioneer, at home in the family museum at Hahei.

own (she had ridden by horse over much of the backblocks of the North Island collecting pledges on behalf of the Women's Christian Temperance Union). At Hahei she helped Horace build home and family and garden. She raised five children; he carved out a dairy farm. For more than half a century she acted as schoolteacher, nurse, postmistress and librarian for the small community that grew up around them. Eventually, in the sixties and seventies, the family subdivided much of their coastal land. The gem on their property, Cathedral Cove north of Hahei, they donated to the nation as a reserve.

When I met them in the 1960s, they were living in contented retirement at Hahei. Horace, an octogenarian, had lost a leg when he walked over an exploding charge of dynamite. But he was still spritely. He had a hut in the bush made from a single horizontal kauri log which he used as an occasional retreat. He had a splendid and exotic garden. But his main occupation and preoccupation was his museum — a marvellously eclectic collection of local, national and international artifacts, relics, natural history specimens and memorabilia stored in what had been the back verandah of the family home. Horace loved to lecture visitors on the significance and uses of each item, especially the Maori tools which were discovered as the sand dunes eroded nearby. Florence, politely but (I felt) a little tight-lipped on occasions, was sent for when it was time for tea and scones.

Horace and Florence Harsant, at the Cook Bicentenary celebrations in Mercury Bay.

When I rediscovered her, Florence was on her own and approaching 90. And how she had blossomed. She had written a book on her early life (*They Called Me Te Maari*), she had broadcast, she had written stories for women's and country magazines. She received the visitors by herself now and was alble to talk uninterruptedly, free from the regimen of a slightly authoritarian partner. We heard more of the women's experience of pioneer life: of the improvised recipes, of children's illnesses and accidents, of taking baths in galvanised tubs and water heated on the wood stove, of boiling clothes in kerosene tins and rinsing them in the creek.

Florence remained in her own domain at Hahei until her 100th year, sustaining what was by now a large community with her knowledge, her good humour and her wisdom. She was herself sustained by the visits of children and grandchildren, the National Radio programme and, as her sight began to fail, the talking books sent to her by the Foundation For the Blind. Her 100th birthday was not simply a commemoration of a wondrous life; it was also a celebration of the rural and Coromandel rituals and values that she had preached and practised all her life. There were Maori and Pakeha present (and both languages spoken). The tables groaned with seafood and country cooking. The speeches were warm, direct, sincere. There was much singing ('Oh, You Beautiful Doll . . .'). There was even more laughter. Two years later Florence still presided as matriarch of the Coromandel, but now from a rest home in Thames.

The late 1960s and early 1970s had brought to the Coromandel an influx of emissaries of the so-called counter-culture. These people, attracted by the climate, the cheap land and the wilderness areas, were largely refugees from the cities and suburbs. They said they were looking consciously for a way of life and a set of values that provided an alternative to the materialist, acquisitive and individualist ethic of Pakeha society. They were dangerous, according to James K Baxter, not because they coveted other people's property and careers, but because they did not. For the most part they lived from sub-sistence farming on communally owned land. Many also turned to craft work, especially weaving and pottery. Others became writers, builders and fisherfolk.

I knew some of these people too from earlier times. Veronica Black had been a childhood neighbour at Paremata. She was now living with her husband and children in the Puhi Community near Colville. A Wellington friend, Felicity Glover, had gone to Colville with friends to build that most potent symbol of the times, a geodesic dome. We failed to find it, and Felicity herself had long since moved on to Canada. But the Colville district retained a largish population of current and former commune members and what was surely the best-stocked country store in the world, run by a co-operative. Dan Hansen's Wilderland Community near Whitianga still flourished, offering an earthy lifestyle complemented by discipline and hard work — and a successful orchard, market garden and apiary.

Up at Driving Creek behind Coromandel township Barry Brickell was turning out the astonishingly beautiful pottery that was the source of his international reputation. He was also building a railway. Initially, it was designed to bring clay and wood down from the hill to his workshop and kiln. Later it became a project in itself: a means of travelling through a historically significant part of the peninsula and observing the healing of the landscape, which Barry was promoting assiduously by replanting trees native to the area.

'It's difficult not to be a conservationist on the Coromandel,' he told us. 'Because to live here is to be conscious of the terrible and thoughtless destruction caused by the extractive industries, timber and gold. This area was devastated by logging. And then the prospectors came along looking for quartz outcrops. The only way they could see them was to keep burning off regenerating trees. And then the mines ripped into the landscape and spewed out their poisonous tailings. Anyone who cares about this place, and who knows how beautiful it was can't help but want to restore it. And then to protect it.'

Another family with whom we re-established joyful contact was the Knights, living on the shore of Wharekawa Harbour, a largely undisturbed estuary that was an important nursery for local fish and native birds. They had built their house among ancient pohutukawas and under the ramparts of an

At Colville, Mecca for commune dwellers: the best-stocked country store in the world.

old Ngati Hei pa, Maungaruawahine. In many ways they were quintessential Coromandel people. They had been conditioned by the counter-culture values of the sixties and seventies. They caught and smoked fish, they grew vegetables, they baked, they made home brew, and they made visitors welcome in their little corner of paradise.

They also exercised what seemed to be the near-eternal vigilance of those who had decided that development on the peninsula had gone far enough. Their harbour had been — and continued to be — a target for a variety of misguided schemes that would forever change its character and appearance: sewage disposal, a marina, intensive subdivisions, a lodge for wealthy members of the Auckland business community. None of these came to fruition. Some failed because they were not financially and commercially viable, others because of the watchfulness of the very active local ratepayers and residents association and their willingness to make costly and time-consuming submissions to the local body and planning authorities.

By the 1980s there was another threat to the peace and wellbeing of the Wharekawa area — and to the peninsula as a whole. The price of gold on the international market had risen spectacularly. Suddenly the claims and the mines abandoned earlier in the century as uneconomic were again the subject of investigation. The highly mechanised character of modern mining made it viable to extract metals which the first wave of gold hunters had had to leave in the ground.

This impending revival of the industry which had caused more environmental damage than any other on the peninsula came at the very stage when the survivors of the hippie migration were becoming more involved in community work; when even the long-established Coromandel families were begin-ning to say that development on the peninsula had gone as far as it should with the building boom of the 1970s. The equation was a recipe for collision and conflict; and the argument for and against mining was to be the most divisive issue on the peninsula for the next decade.

Aware of these nuances, but still drawn strongly by the ethos and history of the Coromandel, we

Barry Brickell, potter, and his bush railway at Driving Creek: an advocate for conservation on a formerly devastated landscape.

bought a section of regenerating bush overlooking a harbour and the sea. Over the next 10 years we built a house and gradually ordered our lives so that it would be possible to live and work there. It is the most sensible and most rewarding decision we have made. We have located ourselves in a place in which we feel in harmony with natural surroundings, and among a community that is attentive to and supportive of the needs of its members.

All the things that excited me about the peninsula as I discovered it 35 years ago through the dusty window of a Wolseley 444 excite me still. Now I see through other windows. In the morning, when I wake, I look in one direction towards a rewarewa tree backdropped by a curtain of tree ferns. Out the other window I see a volcanic escarpment that was once surmounted by a fortified pa. The summit is crowned with pines from an old State Forest planting, the slopes are cloaked in regenerating puriri and pohutukawa. In the foreground stands a grove of gigantic poplar, a relic of the time when the land between us and the sea was farmed. If we stare long enough, we see wood pigeons swoop and loop in spectacular territorial displays. When the windows are open we wake to the calls of the honeyeaters.

It would be possible, from the evidence within sight and sound of those two windows, to deduce much of the Coromandel's natural and human history. The geological features are visible, and the remnants of indigenous flora and fauna. That same view is witness to the peninsula's capacity to recover from past abuse, for this is also a landscape that has been logged, burnt over and mined. In just under 100 years it has reassembled its elements and reasserted the healing powers of nature.

'In the rise of mist from the estuary and the fall of rain,' I wrote recently, 'in the movements of the incoming and outgoing tides, I see a reflection of the deepest mystery and most sustaining pattern in all of life: that of arrival and departure, of death and regeneration.' And, in seeing them, I feel satisfaction. Without being sure of precisely to whom one owes gratitude, I am thankful that this piece of the earth exists and we upon it, to see it and to experience these things.

Lush undergrowth of fern and nikau on the 309 road between Whitianga and Coromandel township.

The Fantail Falls drop in cascades to a deep pool near the 309 road.

Abandoned house and tank stand in view of Castle Rock.

29

Farm buildings under pohutukawas near Waiaro.

Old homesteads at the mouths of narrowing valleys: this one near Waiaro on the Port Jackson Road.

Pakeha settler graves on the edge of the gulf.

Summer resort at Opito Bay.

Remnants of ancient volcanoes dominate the Coromandel skyline. These peaks overlook the Neavesville goldfield inland from Tairua.

Chapter Two
The Long Range of Toi

Uea, uea,
Uea te pu o to whare kia tu tangatanga!
He kapua whakairi naku ki runga o Moehau
Taku kiri ka tokia e te anu matao

Shake, shake
Shake the house to its foundations!
Like the cloud suspended over Moehau
My skin is pierced by cold winds.

Tainui chant

The Coromandel Peninsula sprawls across the eastern side of the Hauraki Gulf like a slumbering leviathan. From Mt Te Aroha to Cape Colville it is 130 kilometres long and — on average — 25 kilometres wide. It reaches more than 900 metres in height. It shelters one of the safest and most popular small boating areas in the world. From the Auckland side of the gulf it is a backdrop redolent of permanence and tranquillity.

It was not always so. The backbone of the range which forms the peninsula was thrust up by volcanic eruptions, the last of which occurred about eight million years ago. Minerals processed in this fierce cauldron precipitated the gemstones and obsidian sought by the Maori for cutting tools and flake knives and the metals sought by Europeans for wealth.

After the lava flows had ceased and solidified, the movement of glaciers and thousands of years of wind and rain sculpted a jagged rampart of peaks and bluffs across a skyline that was to remind later colonists of the islands and highlands of Scotland. The sawing action of rivers and sea scoured out valleys and, on the east coast, scalloped some of the most attractive beaches in the country between high rocky bluffs. Some outlying peninsulas were cut off as islands by the rise and fall and rise of the sea (including the Mercury Islands and Great Barrier which, geologically and botanically, is an extension of the Cormandel), and by the eroding effects of the elements.

Hundreds of thousands of years of undisturbed growth created a rain forest of kauri, rimu and tawa on the upper slopes of the range, the most northerly concentration of alpine plants in New Zealand on Moehau Mountain, and karaka, puriri and pohutukawa groves along the coast. Coromandel kauri were the most southerly colony of these giant trees and they in turn laid down gum as they toppled to earth and deposited their souls of amber while their trunks and branches rotted. In this cycle of growth, decay and growth lay some of the ingredients for the peninsula's boom-and-bust phase in the nineteenth and early twentieth centuries.

Colonies of fauna grew with the trees. A full complement of North Island forest birds assembled,

Whitianga Harbour is a drowned valley system fed by half-a-dozen rivers. Whangapoua is visible over the hill, and the north-east coast.

particularly the honey eaters — the tuis, bellbirds and stitchbirds; and the wattled birds — huia, kokako and saddleback. Bush moas foraged on the forest floor. Native bats found favoured habitats in over-mature trees, especially kauris. Two species of native frog, Archey's and Hochstetter's, among the most primitive of their species in the world, survived through to European times but were rarely seen by Maori or Pakeha. Tuatara, the beaked contemporaries of dinosaurs, lived in cliff burrows until the time of European colonisation, when they were found only on offshore islands.

The coastal margin thronged with waterfowl, waders and seabirds, and seals lived and fished from the rocks between their breeding seasons. The estuaries, rocks and sand beaches were fertile grounds for shellfish, while the waters between the shore and the small islands teemed with snapper, trevally, kahawai, kingfish, mackerel and gurnard. There were larger species too — several kinds of shark were common, while tuna and swordfish cruised further offshore. There were dolphins and porpoises, and migrating humpback whales made their way up and down the east coast.

The first human inhabitants harvested almost all these resources at one time or another. They were the people anthropologists came to call Archaic East Polynesian. We know from their artifacts and ornaments that they came originally from the Society or Marquesas Islands. They may even have been the first settlers in the country. In 1964 archaeologists found a pearl shell fish lure at Tairua that was manufactured in Island Polynesia. It is the only Polynesian artifact found in New Zealand that clearly originates from another country.

These early colonists were hunter-gatherers. They moved around the coast 800 to 1000 years ago, favouring estuaries and river mouths. They lived off birds, including the moa, fish, shellfish and sea mammals. They made their tools from local stone and gemstone cores, and from moa bone. They traded basalt from Tahanga hill near Opito Bay as far north as Houhora and as far south as the Wairarapa coast. Archaeologists have noted that it is the New Zealand stone most like that found in the high volcanic islands of Polynesia. They traded the glass-like Mayor Island obsidian all over the

Tahanga Mountain, which overlooks Opito Bay.
The piles of broken basalt are old moa hunter stone
workshops. Tools made here were traded through much
of the North Island.

North and South Islands and it was carried as far as the Chathams and the Kermadecs.

It was the descendants of these people who later built fortified pa on the peninsula's headlands and grew kumara and taro in the river valleys. According to pan-tribal Maori sources, the traditional name for the peninsula was Te Paeroa A Toi (Toi's long mountain range). It referred to one of the earliest navigators said to have visited the region. Another was Kupe, after whom Whitianga was named (Te Whitianga A Kupe, Kupe's crossing). And still another was Hauraki, 'arid north wind', referring to land bordering the gulf on the western side of the peninsula.

One indication of the seminal nature of early settlement of the peninsula is the fact that the Maori name for Great Mercury Island, Ahuahu, features in the migration stories of Waikato, Bay of Plenty and East Coast tribes. This factor and the evidence of early horticulture on the island — which had an excellent microclimate for the growing of root crops — has led one ethnologist to argue that Great Mercury may have been the traditional Hawaiiki or source for much subsequent Maori migration to other parts of New Zealand.

The era of tribal settlement on the Coromandel was said to have begun with the arrival of the Arawa canoe, whose captain Tamatekapua laid claim to the northern part of the peninsula by announcing that he wished to be buried there, on Moehau Mountain (Moengahau

The head of the Manaia Harbour, fringed with pa sites and mangroves.

Remains of a Maori fish trap near Colville. This arrangement of rocks caught fish, especially flounder, on the falling tide.

Kanuka on the hills above Manaia Harbour.

A Tamatekapua, the windy sleeping place of Tamatekapua). According to tradition this request was carried out by his kinsfolk. Two of them, his brother Hei and his grandson Huarere, brought back to the region followers who intermarried with descendants of the original inhabitants and formed the tribes which occupied the peninsula exclusively until the middle of the sixteenth century AD: Ngati Hei, Ngati Huarere, Ngati Hako and others.

These people, the tangata whenua of the Coromandel, gave names to many of its features (Mercury Bay, for example, was Te Whanganui a Hei, the great harbour of Hei, and a settlement to the south was Te O a Hei, the exclamation of Hei, known to a later generation as Hahei). The peninsula as a whole they likened to a giant canoe with its stern at Moehau, its bow at Mt Te Aroha and its mooring ropes stretching into the Kaimais ('ko Moehau ki raro, Te Aroha ki runga, rere atu ki te Kaokaoroa-a-Patetere').

From the middle of the sixteenth century they came under attack from Tainui tribes from the west, originally from Waikato. Led by Marutuahu from Kawhia, these intruders moved on to the peninsula from the Hauraki Plains and claimed traditional rights by virtue of the fact that the Tainui canoe had also visited the region at about the same time as the Arawa and left place names acknowledged by the local people. Marutuahu and his sons — Tamatepo, Tamatera, Whanaunga and Te Ngako — began a campaign against the tangata whenua tribes that was to be carried on over four generations.

From this martial holocaust only Ngati Hei and Ngati Hako survived with their separate mana and identity intact. The remainder of the tangata whenua people were absorbed by the Tainui victors, who formed the Marutuahu confederation of tribes: Ngati Maru, Ngati Tamatera, Ngati Whanaunga and Ngati Paoa.

By the late eighteenth and early nineteenth centuries, Ngati Hei's territory had contracted to the coastline from Kuaotunu to Tairua. Bay of Plenty tribes were threatening them from the south and Ngapuhi began attacking from the north. After Ngapuhi had suffered at least one defeat at the hands of Ngati Hei on Mahurangi Island off Hahei, Hongi Hika led the northern tribes back to the region with muskets in the 1820s and came close to exterminating the tangata whenua at Wharekaho Beach. Twenty survivors took refuge in the so-called Hole in the Wall at Tauhinu. They and their chiefs Hinganoa and Repana were the ancestors of the few Ngati Hei who remained to deal with Europeans and sell land at Mercury Bay and Tairua later in the century. Other Ngati Hei remnants fled from what they now saw as vulnerable seaside pa and took refuge inland. Some intermarried with Tainui and Bay of Plenty tribes.

Hongi Hika's warriors also defeated a large number of Ngati Maru at Totara Pa near the present town of Thames in December 1821. They made as if to attack the pa and then seemed to relent. Instead, they were given all the taonga or tribal treasures that Ngati Maru could assemble. They then left with these, claiming a symbolic victory, and camped at Tararu further up the coast. Late that night, with the defenders off their guard and celebrating a reprieve, Ngapuhi returned and slaughtered the inhabitants of Te Totara, an act of subterfuge that still rankles among the descendants of Coromandel tribes.

Later in the nineteenth century, the pattern of Maori colonisation was complicated still further by the gift of the Hauraki tribes to Ngati Porou of land at Kennedy's

The meeting house Hotunui, built by Ngati Awa at Parawai, Thames, as a gift for the Ngati Maru chief Taipari.

Bay and Mataora Bay. This came about partly in thanks for assistance in the fighting against Ngapuhi and partly to give them ports of call for their trading vessels; and by the settlement of other East Coast Maori on other parts of the peninsula, such as Tairua. In the 1880s, Arawa survivors of the Tarawera eruption were relocated near Tairua, Opoutere and Waihi. Finally, the prospect of forestry work and kauri gum drew Maori from many North Island tribes to work on the peninsula in the late 1800s and early 1900s, and many of them remained.

Despite this complexity, some features of Maori tradition were shared and bequeathed by all Coromandel tribes. One was the use of the earliest place names associated with Toi, Kupe and Hei. Another was the sacred nature of Te Moehau, the northern summit of the range where Tamatekapua was reputed to lie. Yet another was the belief in Mahoao or wild men of the bush. Edward Tregear, working as a surveyor on the peninsula in the nineteenth century, recorded what Ngati Whanaunga Maori told him one night when he was camped near Castle Rock above Coromandel township: 'The Maoris insisted that the locality in which we were was haunted by . . . fierce white-skinned creatures like men but of great stature, their mouths having gleaming tusks, their heads shaggy with matted yellow hair. These beings roamed about in this enchanted forest, calling out "Haere-mai! haere-mai!"

Maori houses at Ponga Flat near Thames in the 1860s.

(Come hither! come hither!) and, if obeyed, would devour their victims.'

This tradition was corrupted by Maori and Pakeha jokesters in the twentieth century, until it spoke of a so-called 'Moehau monster', which lived in the deepest recesses of the forest and appeared periodically to terrorise bushmen. Alleged sightings of the creature became an annual story for local newspapers during the silly season and a favourite leg-pull with which residents would alarm visitors, especially women. (In the 1980s it was announced that a television crew, capitalising on what was described as worldwide interest, was being sent from Japan to find and film the 'Moehau Monster' and to study it for scientific purposes. The expedition failed to arrive in New Zealand.)

By the latter part of the twentieth century, the vestiges of Ngati Hei in Whitianga and Tairua were recognised as tangata whenua and spiritual guardians of the eastern side of the peninsula (it was they who vetoed the re-sinking of the *Rainbow Warrior* off Slipper Island, one of their traditional urupa, in 1985). The Tainui-based Hauraki tribes, including Ngati Maru and Ngati Whanaunga, are tangata whenua along much of the western side. A mixed Tainui-Bay of Plenty settlement at Manaia, which includes Ngati Whanaunga and Ngati Pukenga (gifted land there in the 1850s in return for assistance in earlier tribal fighting), is now the largest Maori community on the peninsula north of Thames. A Ngati Porou settlement and marae survive at Kennedy's Bay, and there is a small mixed tribal settlement, largely Tainui, at Opoutere. Whangamata has a tribally mixed community and plans a marae. Waihi has a marae supported by some of the Ngati Porou families who formerly lived at Mataora Bay. Thames has a large Maori population and a major marae, Matai Whetu, and is regarded as headquarters of Ngati Maru.

Buddy Mikaere of Manaia has written an account of what it means to him to be tangata whenua on the peninsula:

'There are reminders everywhere. I can see on the skyline above the valley the Tomo, the rock fortress, still standing guard. When the day is clear, you can stand on the top defences and command a warrior's

Joshua Wilson and Dave Brown, Ngati Porou descendants on the beach below tribal land at Mataora.

view. Towards the tip of the peninsula, the blue bulk of Moehau shoulders the horizon — the burial mountain of chiefs and heroes. To the south are the remnant forests of the Manaia sanctuary, where the last of the kokako sing to the last of the giant kauri.

'In the bush below the fortress is the cave where our bones lie, and a landslide has uncovered a great midden of shells several feet thick on the slopes of the pa. Down by my father's bach is the little hollow where my great-grandfather, Taoki, had his whare, and that little terrace on the hillside, sited to catch groundwater, is where he grew kumara. The deep narrow foot-track winding through the manuka stands is the daily path he and others walked to fetch springwater. The humble little basalt adzes which I keep in a drawer were found by my mother under the Manaia blackberries. When I pick up these adzes, they speak of the unbridgeable gulf between my ancestors and me. But if I hold them long enough, they start to spin a dream of the people who make me real.'

The first Europeans known to have seen the peninsula, and to have recorded information about its appearance and Maori inhabitants, were the crew of James Cook's barque *Endeavour*, which sailed up the east coast early in November 1769. After renaming the Mayor and Aldermen Islands, Cook and his men entered Mercury Bay on 3 November. Fascinatingly, and unusually, we also have a Maori account of this visit. The Ngati Whanaunga chief Horeta Te Taniwha, who was a child at the time, lived long enough to record his recollection of this momentous event.

'. . . when our old men saw the ship they said it was an atua, a god, and the people on board were tupua, strange beings or "goblins". The ship came to anchor, and the boats pulled on shore. As our old men looked at the manner in which they came on shore, the rowers pulling with their backs to the bows of the boat, the old people said, "yes, it is so: these people are goblins; their eyes are at the back of their heads . . ." When these goblins came on shore we (the women and children) . . . ran away from them into the forest . . . but, as the goblins stayed some time, and did not do any evil to

'Spöring's Grotto' — an engraving based on Herman Spöring's sketch of the
Ngati Hei pa Te Puta O Paretauhinu, Mercury Bay, November 1769.

our braves, we came back one by one, and gazed at them, and we stroked their garments with our hands, and we were pleased with the whiteness of their skins . . .

'There was one supreme man in that ship. We knew that he was the lord of the whole by his perfect gentlemanly and noble demeanour. He seldom spoke, but some of the goblins spoke much . . . all that he did was to handle our mats and hold our mere, spears and waha-ika, and touch the hair of our heads. He was a very good man, and came to us — the children — and patted our cheeks, and gently touched our heads.'

Most of the people living in the bay at this time were Ngati Hei. But there were others from other tribes, such as Horeta Te Taniwha's group, who moved from place to place around the peninsula, gathering food and keeping their own rights of occupation and use alive. On the whole they greeted the English sailors in friendship, supplied them with fish and shellfish, and helped them find wood and fresh water and other supplies, such as the wild celery which Cook had boiled and served to his crew to prevent scurvy.

Cook had the *Endeavour* heeled and the hull scrubbed while he was in the bay. On 9 November he assisted his astronomer to observe the transit of Mercury across the face of the sun, which in turn allowed him to determine New Zealand's longitude (and the position of Mercury Bay became the pivot for Cook's chart of the whole country). Near the same stretch of shore, on Cook's Beach alongside the Purangi River, the navigator claimed possession of the surrounding countryside in the name of King George III.

Having called the bay Mercury in commemoration of the planet's transit, Cook explored it further. He took his botanist Joseph Banks and others in two boatloads four or five miles up the Whitianga River. Here they found kauri gum stuck to the mangroves — and assumed incorrectly that it was extruded from this plant — water fowl and wading birds, and banks of cockles, scallops and oysters. They also stopped briefly at the ruins of Whitianga pa, which had once been the settlement of Hei.

The mouth of the Waihou, which James Cook called The Thames. The English name now attaches to the town on the east side of the river which Cook used to reach stands of kahikatea miles inland.

The cemented landing on the Cook's Beach side of Whitianga Harbour covers the stone blocks of the oldest suriving wharf in the country.

Two days later some of the Englishmen visited two pa on the north side of the bay. One was a small and picturesque settlement built over an arched rock, which they called Spöring's Grotto after the party's assistant naturalist, who sketched it. The other was Wharetaewa. Banks' and Cook's description of this position is the most detailed ever made of an eighteenth-century fortified pa and was of considerable assistance to archaeologists investigating the site nearly 200 years later, and to Ngati Hei descendants gathering information about their history and heritage.

The *Endeavour* sailed on around the top of the peninsula and Cook named the cape after Lord Colville, his old friend and former naval commander. The barque then tracked down the west coast as far as Te Puru. On the following day, 20 November, the Englishmen took two boats to the head of the bay, where Cook found the mouth of the Waihou River. He named it the Thames on account of its resemblance to the great English waterway.

The boats then rowed 12 to 14 miles up the Waihou — the furthest journey inland that Cook was to make in New Zealand. He and Banks were astonished by what they found. 'The banks . . . were compleatly cloathd with the finest timber my Eyes ever beheld,' wrote the botanist. They disembarked on the west bank of the river near Hikutaia and walked into a dense forest of kahikatea. Cook noted: ' . . . we had not gone a hundred yards into the Woods before we found a tree that girted 19 feet 8 Inches, 6 feet above the Ground, and having a quadrant with me I found its length from the root to the first branch to be 89 feet, it was as streight as an arrow and taper'd but very little in proportion to its length, so that I judged that there was 356 solid feet of timber in this tree clear of the branches. We saw many others of the same sort several of which were taller than the one we measured and all of them very stout . . .'

It was this description which brought the next European vessel to the district. It led also to an intensive export trade in Coromandel kauri and kahikatea, and to the beginnings of the whole timber industry in New Zealand.

Twenty five years later, in the summer of 1794/95, Captain Dell and the crew of the ship *Fancy* came to the Waihou from Port Jackson in New South Wales. Their commission was to find spars for the naval vessels of the East India Company. They camped up the river at a site they called Graves End, known now to be Hikutaia, and they felled and loaded 213 kahikatea spars up to 140 feet in length. They were welcomed by the local Ngati Maru and Ngati Paoa people, who assisted in the work and supplied the sailors with food.

Over the next six years at least five more vessels returned to the Waihou for identical cargoes. They too were assisted by local Maori, who also traded flax and potatoes. By 1799 there were four Europeans at Hikutaia, helping to organise the sale of Maori labour and the trade. They lived as Maori, took Maori wives, and were the first of that species who came to be known in the nineteenth century as 'Pakeha-Maori'.

The trading with Maori for the export of timber gathered momentum as the nineteenth century advanced. In 1820 the Royal Naval storeship *Coromandel* gave its name to Waiau Harbour, halfway down the west side of the peninsula, and ultimately to the township that grew up there and to the peninsula itself. That same vessel also brought Samuel Marsden of the Anglican Church Missionary Society, who landed near the mouth of the Waihou, preached to local Maori, and then made

Coromandel Harbour with Castle Rock on the skyline, from a sketch by Charles Heaphy in the 1840s.

54

his way overland to Tauranga and other Bay of Plenty communities.

Contact between Maori and Pakeha on the Coromandel — and between Pakeha and Pakeha — was by no means always harmonious. The brig *Venus*, seized by mutineers in Sydney in 1806, is believed to have been captured and burned by Ngati Tamatera at Harataunga, later known as Kennedy's Bay, after its crew had kidnapped Maori women around the peninsula. Two other ships, the *Trial* and the *Brothers*, were attacked in the same bay by Ngapuhi in 1816 for refusing to pay for a cargo of flax loaded at the Bay of Islands. Over 200 Ngapuhi and local Ngati Tamatera are said to have been killed in this engagement by the swivel canons which cleared both vessels of attackers and then bombarded Maori on the shore. Even John Kennedy, an early Pakeha-Maori resident after whom the bay was eventually named, perished in violent circumstances. He was murdered by his Australian crew and his boat scuttled when he tried to deliver a cargo of goods and money to Auckland in 1843.

In 1840, when the Scottish doctor and entrepreneur John Logan Campbell lived for a time at Herekino on the shore of Coromandel Harbour, the peninsula and its inhabitants were involved in regular and well-organised trade with vessels and companies operating out of Sydney. Campbell stayed with a Pakeha-Maori named William Webster, who had married the daughter of Horeta Te Taniwha, the Ngati Whanaunga chief who remembered Cook.

'He had many irons in the fire,' Campbell noted of Webster. 'He built small schooners, prepared cargoes of timber for the Australian colonies with Native labour, he had traders located far and wide amongst the Natives buying up their produce — flax, potatoes, pigs; latter were "salted down" and casked and when he had sufficient to make a small cargo he shipped it off to Sydney.' Later, in the peninsula's coastal valleys, Campbell saw 'great fields of maize and potatoes' planted by local Maori for this export trade.

With the transfer of the nation's capital to the shore of the Waitemata in September 1840, these ventures expanded even more intensively. Major trading posts opened at Mercury Bay and Tairua.

Most of Auckland's supplies of early meat, dried fish, vegetables, fruit and firewood came from the Coromandel. And it was Coromandel timber, especially kauri, that built a large portion of the new town's homes and commercial and official buildings. Without the resources of the peninsula, Auckland would have developed far more slowly than it did.

In 1853, William Swainson, the colony's second Attorney-General, wrote that large quantities of produce continued to flow into Auckland from the Coromandel. Fleets of up to 40 large canoes would sail into the Waitemata perhaps twice a year and set up a market on the foreshore. 'Pigs and potatoes, wheat, maize, melons, grapes, pumpkins, onions, flax, turkeys, geese, ducks, fowls and firewood are exposed for sale in great abundance and meet with a ready market.' Eight years later, the shipping columns of the newspaper *The New Zealander* listed 48 boats arriving in Auckland from Cabbage Bay on the peninsula carrying timber, firewood and house blocks in addition to wheat, maize and potatoes.

Even as the Coromandel timber boom gathered momentum, another was in the making. Visiting whalers found traces of gold there in 1842. Ten years later a timber merchant, Charles Ring, claimed a $1000 reward offered by the Auckland provincial government for the discovery of a 'payable' gold-field in the province. Ring had noticed gold-bearing quartz embedded in a log which he had tumbled down a riverbed behind Coromandel Harbour. Subsequent prospecting turned up further deposits of the precious metal and the peninsula's first gold-rush was under way: around Coromandel township and at Cape Colville and Mercury Bay.

In spite of the circumstances of its discovery, Coromandel gold was largely underground in quartz veins. It was difficult and expensive to extract. The first 'rush' lasted little more than a year before potential miners turned their attention elsewhere, particularly to the South Island, where the Otago and West Coast gold-fields proved to be extensive, alluvial and rich. By the late 1860s the Coromandel claims were being worked again, however, and partnerships and companies were formed to raise capital for the installation of stamper batteries, which crushed quartz and separated out the gold.

Most of this activity centred on Thames, Waihi and Coromandel townships. Other communities were to spring up at Waikino, Karangahake, Waitekauri and Kuaotunu. By 1871 there were 693 batteries operating around Thames alone, shaking the settlement day and night as if from a continuous earthquake. It was Waihi that turned out to be the most productive of these boom towns, disgorging bullion worth four billion dollars between 1879 and 1952 and employing 1500 men in the Martha Mine at its peak. The total production of Coromandel gold in the late nineteenth and early twentieth centuries was 43,800,000 ounces of bullion worth around six billion dollars.

The presence of gold was also the factor that enabled successive governments to wrest much of the land on the Coromandel from Maori to Crown and European ownership. Large tracts were leased for purposes of mining, regardless of whether or not they contained gold, and these became in effect leases in perpetuity. Other sections of the peninsula, particularly the high slopes, were taken under the Crown's Wastelands Act.

Maori objections to this process of alienation were raised fruitlessly with successive governments, and discussed at the Kotahitanga (Maori Parliament) meetings in the 1890s. One local chief, Hamiora Mangakahia of Ngati Whanaunga, was elected premier of Kotahitanga in 1892.

One of the earliest goldfield hotels, the Tokatea, on the hill above Coromandel township.

Above: Karangahake in 1914, one of the half a dozen Coromandel towns that vanished when the gold ran out. Compare this with the contemporary photograph of the three or four surviving houses and buildings.

His wife Meri, another national Maori leader, left their home at Whangapoua the following year to lobby the movement for the emancipation of Maori women.

Throughout the gold-mining years the demand for Coromandel timber remained high. Bushmen built dams far up the peninsula's valleys to build up water pressure and shoot logs down riverbeds to the coast. Millions of superfeet of timber, principally kauri, were removed in this manner between 1880 and the 1920s. Much of it was cut up at Coromandel, Tairua and Mercury Bay, but even communities as small as Kennedy's Bay and Whangapoua had mills. Vast rafts of logs were also towed to Great Barrier Island and to Auckland for processing. When accessible kauri was gone, bushmen turned to other trees. Once logged, many of the surviving cut-over forests were torched.

It was at about this time that the region discovered an identity of its own. Maori residents on the peninsula had always felt

A miner's funeral in Karangahake shortly before the First World War.

The solidity of the Bank of New Zealand facade in Thames in the late 1860s contrasts with the frontier character of the streets.

The grandeur of the Brian Boru Hotel, Thames, built in 1868.

an identification with the place, a feeling hallowed by a knowledge of its history, place-names and the association of their ancestors with the land and the events which had taken place on it. Now, from the late nineteenth century, in spite of the scattered and isolated nature of Coromandel households and settlements, Pakeha residents too began to feel a special association with one another and with the region in which they lived and worked.

This new feeling became apparent in the manner in which they raised troops for the war in South Africa and paraded them proudly through Coromandel, Thames and Waihi before their departure. It was apparent in mourning ceremonies for Queen Victoria and celebrations for the coronation of Edward VII. And it was apparent in the rough-and-tumble of local politics which produced some outstanding unionists and national politicians, such as Alfred Cadman, Bill Parry and Tim Armstrong, who always attributed their success

Thames in the late nineteenth century, third largest town in the country.

to the apprenticeships they served in the peninsula's timber and mining communities. (Another such politician was Harry Holland, first parliamentary leader of the New Zealand Labour Party, who came to the Coromandel from Australia in 1912 to help miners waging the Waihi strike.)

With the exception of the operation of the Martha Mine, which continued until 1952 (and reopened in 1988), the region's gold and timber bonanza was largely over by the time of the First World War. Towns began to shrink. Some, like Waikino and Waitekauri, virtually disappeared. Those that survived did so either by servicing the trade in kauri gum, which had only another two decades to run; or by the slow growth of farming, fishing, exotic forestry and tourism. The mountainous interior was largely abandoned again to nature. Scars left by mining, logging and fires were slowly covered by regenerating vegetation. Pockets of virgin kauri and other native trees did survive, but only on the ridges and in the least accessible valleys.

Mixed farming by Pakeha settlers had begun in the peninsula's valleys and coastal flats, and on the Hauraki Plains, in the 1860s. By the 1880s the development of dairying was well under way and grew to account for more than 60 per cent of the region's farming income. Nearly a third came from sheep runs on the more hilly country, and about 10 per cent from beef cattle.

The advance of the twentieth century

Finding an identity: the local contingent leaves for the South African War from the township of Coromandel, 1899.

brought a dramatic expansion of fishing out of the ports of Thames, Coromandel, Whitianga and Whangamata until by the 1980s it was generating around $25 million per year. The region also contributed 10 per cent of the national catch of the country's favourite fish, snapper. Oyster and mussel farming were well developed by the 1990s and contributing 20 per cent of the national harvest of these shellfish. The region's scallop beds were the largest in the country.

Another farming option taken up more widely on the peninsula in the 1970s and 1980s was horticulture. The number of orchards and market gardens expanded dramatically, and kiwifruit farming became attractive in the light of the adjacent Bay of Plenty boom in that crop. Grape growing and wine making joined a growing list of local horticulture-based activities.

During the Great Depression a further major industry was established in an effort to provide employment and make use of burnt-over bush: exotic forests. Plantings of pines, eucalypts, macrocarpa, larch, oaks and other broadleaf trees commenced in the Tairua and Maramarua Forests in 1930. The second phase was begun in 1960 and, in addition to Tairua and Maramarua, took in Moehau, Waikawau, Whangapoua, Maratoto, Hikuai and Kauaeranga. These later plantings were almost exclusively of radiata pine and (to a lesser extent) Douglas fir. By the 1980s mature trees were providing steady

Collecting and bagging farmed mussels at Te Kouma, between Manaia and Coromandel.

employment for forestry workers and millers, initially at the direction of the New Zealand Forest Service and later — after privatisation — largely under Carter Holt Harvey Ltd. The peninsula had around 20,000 hectares in exotic forest as against the remaining 85,000 in indigenous bush, most of it managed by the Department of Conservation.

The other important growth industry has been tourism. The region's marvellous beaches, good fishing grounds (which Zane Grey helped to popularise after catching game fish out of Mercury Bay in the 1920s and 1930s), native forests, gemstones, the spectacular juxtapositions of hills and sea, and the evidence of its Maori, mining and milling past — all this has remained an enticing menu for visitors, especially in the summer months. The building of the Kopu-Hikuai highway in the 1960s and the upgrading of the eastern coastal roads had the effect of opening up the most appealing parts of the peninsula to intensive holiday traffic.

The towns of Thames, Coromandel, Whitianga, Tairua and Whangamata now depend on visitors' income over the holiday season to keep them economically and socially viable. Some communities, such as Whangamata, Onemana, Pauanui and Whangapoua, are largely products of the demand for holiday and retirement homes. By the 1990s, more than one and a half million people lived within 160 kilometres of the peninsula; more than half a million visited the Coromandel each summer. And those numbers were increasing.

All of which, while a source of optimism for Coromandel residents, also sounds a warning. It may prove difficult to preserve the natural and historical character of the region while, at the same time, catering adequately for growing hordes of visitors. It may be even more difficult to achieve the right balance if the mining industry succeeds in re-establishing itself on a large scale, with detrimental consequences for the environment and for economic activities, such as tourism and fishing, which are dependent on the environment. And it is this set of issues that is the most fertile source of public debate and controversy on the peninsula in the 1990s.

A mussel farm near the entrance to Manaia Harbour; Coromandel Harbour beyond.

A typical Coromandel farm: a pocket of pasture in a fold in the hills on the road to Port Charles.

Dairy cows graze the flats of the Hikuai Valley.

Olive Forsman of Ngati Pukenga in her garden at Manaia.

The shell of the Ringatu church abandoned and declared tapu at Paritu near Opoutere.

The old Wharekawa Native School, built in 1908 and now the Opoutere Youth Hostel.

At school at Manaia, the Ngati Whanaunga and Ngati Pukenga settlement
that is now the largest Maori community north of Thames.

Ringatu meeting house south of Tairua. This was a place of worship and burial for a community which had originated on the East Coast.

Interior of All Saints Church, Manaia.

Buddy Mikaere of Ngati Pukenga on the shore of tribal fishing ground, Manaia Harbour.

The granite wharf at Paritu, close to the quarry which provided stone for dozens of public buildings throughout the country, including Parliament and its Beehive extension.

Memorial to local soldiers who died abroad in two world wars, outside the old county council building in Coromandel township. The plinth is Coromandel granite.

The Coromandel volcanic rampart, which has no counterpart elsewhere in New Zealand, dominates pasture in the Hikuai Valley.

Cattle on the move to coastal pasture near Fantail Bay on the Port Jackson road.

Farm buildings and holiday homes at Kirita Bay south of Manaia.

Anthea Ward, Moehau farmer, with her working dogs.

A fishing boat from an earlier era rots among the mangroves in Manaia Harbour.

A colony of mainly English trees on the banks of the Tairua River.

Commercial fishing boat in
Whangamata Harbour, Clark Island
or Hauturu behind.

Crayfish pots await collection from one of the wharves at Whangapoua Harbour.

Pioneer stone cottage, enlarged in wood, at Fantail Bay, Moehau.

Homestead remains on the Colville–Coromandel road.

The Colville War Memorial Hall, community centre for an earlier generation of farming families.

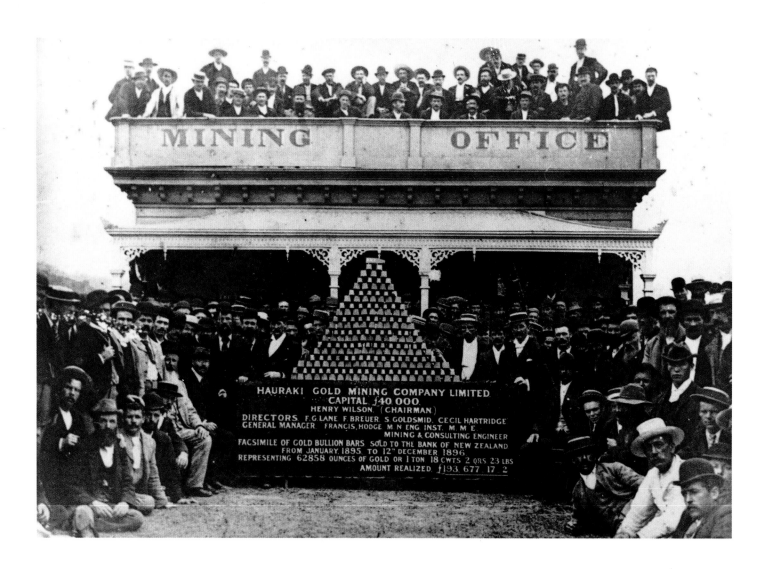

Directors and miners of the Hauraki Gold Mining Company celebrate two bonanza years of bullion production in Coromandel in 1896. Because of the expense of the machinery required for mining, crushing and mineral extraction, the industry was heavily dependent on investment from Auckland and London.

CHAPTER THREE

BONANZA DAYS

The richest reefs of Bendigo
They say can't hold a candle,
Unto the claims at Driving Creek
Down there on the Coromandel.

Charles Thatcher,
music hall song (1862)

Enormous columns of straight unknotted wood. These kauri off the 309 road demonstrate why the tree was irresistable to loggers and timber merchants.

Coromandel Peninsula boomed in the last three decades of the nineteenth century when timber extraction and gold mining were at their height. Indeed, by the late 1870s, Thames was the third largest centre in the country, behind Auckland and Dunedin, and many people believed it was destined to become the largest and the nation's commercial capital. Even Waihi was to make the list of New Zealand's 12 biggest towns. Peninsula politicians, such as Alfred Cadman (who became, appropriately enough, Minister of Mines) boasted that their region was the most prosperous in the country — some said in the British Empire. They may have been right. And their confidence was buoyed up by visible wealth and Victorian notions of progress. But it was a prosperity based on finite resources. It was a bubble whose very inflation guaranteed that it was destined to burst.

The removal of timber from the peninsula, which had begun with the East India Company expeditions to the Waihou in the late eighteenth century, gathered pace after the visit of the naval store-ship *Coromandel* in 1820. The first traders took kahikatea and flax. From the 1820s the favoured cargo was kauri, harder and more durable than kahikatea, and in demand in Britain for shipbuilding because of the diminution of Baltic pine. Kauri was also present on the Coromandel in far greater quantity than any other timber because of the prodigious size of the mature trees.

Kauri are not the largest trees in the world, nor do they grow to be the oldest. The Californian sequoias claim both titles. But the New Zealand kauri comes second, and the largest ever recorded stood on the Coromandel Peninsula.

One tree growing at the head of Mill Creek in Mercury Bay in the 1840s was estimated to have a girth of 23.77 m and a height to the first branch of 24.3 metres (by way of comparison, the largest kauri standing today, Tane Mahuta in the Waipoua Forest, has a girth of 13.77 m and a trunk height of 17.68 m). This specimen, the largest recorded, was found dead in the 1850s, apparently killed by lightning. Another Mercury Bay giant, also from Mill Creek, was felled in the 1870s without measurement. Its stump, however, used subsequently for bush dances and as a band rotunda, had a diameter of 7.3 metres. The botanist Thomas Kirk estimated its age at more than 4000 years. A tree near the Tararu Creek just north of Thames was never measured officially. But 'common knowledge' in the area in the 1860s and 1870s gave it a girth of 26.82 metres, which made it the largest ever reported.

Not every one of the hundreds of thousands of trees felled on the peninsula in the nineteenth century was a giant. But it was common for kauri logs to have volumes of between 100 and 200 square metres. And trunks of this magnitude required careful and skilful handling.

The first kauri taken, of course, were those growing close to the shore of navigable harbours: in Coromandel Harbour, Mercury Bay and Tairua, and near the mouth of the Waihou. They were used for shipbuilding in Britain (carried most often in ships travelling via Port Jackson in New South Wales) and for ships, houses and buildings in the Australian colonies. By the 1840s Coromandel kauri was contributing to the building of Auckland, and a little later to the construction of almost every other major town in the North Island. In the 1870s builders from as far away as the Chatham Islands sent for Coromandel timber. A heavy quantity was also dispatched to the west coast of North America; it was said that the huge fire which followed the 1906 San Francisco earthquake destroyed more Coromandel kauri than was ever burned by a New Zealand conflagration.

Coromandel bushmen in front of their shanty with a kauri that has been scarfed in preparation for sawing.

The business of felling huge trees was itself complex and dangerous. The trunk would be scarfed by axemen to determine the direction in which it would fall. It would then be cut with a cross-cut saw, usually from the side opposite the scarf, with one or two men pulling from each end. This could take half a day in the case of a large tree. Once down the trunk had to be trimmed of branches and further cross-sawn to reduce it to a number of movable logs. These in turn were 'sniped' by axe (rounded at the edges) to make them easier to slide, or squared off for more secure placement on tram or railway vehicles, which carried them to the nearest waterway.

Accidents could and did occur at every part of the process. Sometimes trees toppled in unexpected directions and crushed loggers. Sometimes falling giants brought down other trees or branches which caused injury. Sometimes axes ricocheted and saws buckled and jumped. Sometimes limbs were pinned or crushed when logs were being rolled or slid. Many a bushman was forced to retire after the loss of a hand, an arm or a leg; others made their last journey straight from the forest to the peninsula's cemeteries.

It was after the more accessible trees were felled that the industry became more organised and more ingenious in its methods. In some parts of the peninsula logs were hauled from the slopes and river flats by teams of bullocks and horses. In other valleys tramways were built, initially

A sniped kauri log is jacked into position for removal at Simpson's Beach, Mercury Bay.

Oxen haul a kauri log out of the bush near Whitianga

Bush railways provide a highly efficient method of moving logs from the forest to the coast.

A bush dam in the Tairua watershed, 1880s. The uprights take the weight of logs and water; the gate is between the rectangular supports at right.

A chained raft of logs in the Whenuakite River near Coroglen awaits removal to the Kauri Timber Company's mill at Mercury Bay.

using wooden rails and wheels, later iron. Very often these worked solely on gravity. They were replaced in some areas in the late nineteenth century by miniature railways using small locomotives to pull log-laden trucks.

The most ingenious method of getting logs down to the coast from the higher ridges and valleys involved the damming of streams and rivers. Trees were felled, cut up, then jacked, rolled or slid into riverbeds. These waterways were blocked with wooden dams built from adjacent trees. Once considerable pressure had built up behind the dams they were tripped and the sudden surge of water carried logs down the gullies and valleys to the site of a larger dam, where the process was repeated. Those who witnessed such explosions never forgot them. Many were reduced to tears. One Coromandel forest worker, H E Hewlett, wrote this account of a drive in the 1890s:

'. . . [An] uproar arose on the left — the sound of innumerable logs thudding against each other, driven by the violence of the water. Then a wall of water and logs, many feet in height, came into sight and beneath the westering moon we saw thousands of logs go by. They seemed to be alive, grumbling and complaining in their discomfort and agony. Great logs were driven high on the bank, swung around and torn away again. Long logs, their butts driven into the bed of the creek, rose up on end and fell over again, until the whole

The steamer Stella *prepares to tow a raft while the scow* Ngahua *uses derricks to load logs. Much of the Coromandel Peninsula's contact with the wider world in the late nineteenth and early twentieth centuries was dependent on the sail-powered scows.*

93

Maori loggers scull a raft to a storage boom on Wharekawa Harbour, 1890s. Surrounding hills have long since been cleared of forest and burnt over by prospectors and gum collectors.

Opoutere Beach and Wharekawa Harbour: a major nursery ground for Coromandel fish and birds.

A loggers' shanty with paling walls and shingled roof high in the Wharekawa watershed.
The cook stands at front left, alongside a standard sized cross-cut saw.

mighty mass had gone thundering down the main Wharekawa to the salt water, where tugs and scows would get hold of them and take them to the waiting saws in Auckland.'

Some of those waiting saws were closer to hand than Auckland. Charles Ring, the same merchant who discovered gold on the peninsula in 1852, opened a local sawmill at Driving Creek behind the present town of Coromandel in about the same year. Others followed at Kikowakare and Kennedy's Bay. By the 1860s Mercury Bay and Whangapoua had two mills each. More were built at Port Charles, Colville, Coromandel itself, Gumtown, Tiki and Mahakirau. All initially used pit saws; machine-driven saws began to make their appearance from the late nineteenth century in the larger mills, such as that run by the Kauri Timber Company at Whitianga. Initially, they processed almost exclusively kauri. As supplies of this wood began to diminish, the loggers turned their attention to rimu, miro, tawa and totara. Kauri was the backbone of the industry, however, and when accessible supplies were exhausted by the 1920s, the timber industry on the Coromandel collapsed.

By the 1990s there was still virgin kauri bush on the peninsula. But it stood in places which had been far too difficult to log in the days of the timber boom; hence much of it is not easy to reach even now. One such stand is in the Moehau Ecological Area of the Coromandel Forest Park; another in the Manaia Forest Sanctuary; and still another in the upper reaches of the Tairua River. All require a tramp of several hours to reach the mature trees. The Manaia and Tairua stands actually contain a greater number of large kauri than the better known Waipoua Forest in Northland. One of the Manaia trees, Tanenui, has a girth of more than 10 metres and is the sixth largest tree in the country. One of the Tairua trees is the ninth largest; and one of its neighbours is the tallest at 56.3 metres.

Other giants are more easily reached. The Devcich kauri, three-quarters of an hour's walk down a signposted track from the top of the Kopu-Hikuai Road, has a girth of 10.54 metres and is 46.5 metres high. The Tapu-Coroglen Road provides access to the Waiomu Ecological Area, which has the largest stand of kauri below an altitude of 300 metres; and the famous 'square' kauri, so named for the flanges that alter the shape of its bole, is close to the same road. Five kilometres north of Tairua the 'twin kauris', each with a girth of around 5 metres, can be viewed from the roadside.

A rich culture grew around the lives of the Coromandel bushmen and died with the trees on which they depended for their living. Gangs employed by timber merchants would go into the forest to build large shanties in the areas in which they planned to work. These buildings, with split paling walls and nikau-thatched roofs, would be home for up to several years. They had bunks around the interior walls, a long table in the centre over an earth floor, and a kitchen and wide fireplace with a wooden or corrugated iron chimney down one end.

For as long as the current contract lasted the men lived, ate, slept and took days off in such quarters. It was largely a womanless society (though some women began working in the camps as cooks in the early twentieth century). In the evenings the loggers read by lamplight and candle, played cards, told stories and sang. Liquor was forbidden in most camps because it led inevitably to trouble — as did spitting, talking about sex and playing cards for money. Alcohol was sought in the bush grog-shanties, especially in the nineteenth century, and in the towns between contracts or on rare holidays; liquor and sometimes sex were indulged in to excess in Thames, Coromandel, Whitianga and Tairua, frequently at the expense of law and order. Although some individuals were unpopular, there was in general a strong camaraderie and sense of honour among bushmen. They prided themselves in working extraordinarily hard and in not stealing from one another; they looked after mates who were sick, injured or sacked; they often assumed responsibilities for bereaved families.

With the bushmen came the gum diggers. From the late nineteenth century these men — they were almost all men on the Coromandel — dug the swamps and river flats, and then entered the forest to root around the base of living trees and around the stumps and trunks of fallen ones. As quality gum became more difficult to find they began to climb to the forks of living trees and to 'bleed' them by slashing wounds from which the gum ran and eventually solidified. This practice, which led to trees becoming diseased, was banned in the twentieth century. But there was nobody to police the ban.

Kauri gum was in demand for the preparation of varnish, linoleum and dental supplies. The periods when the demand was strongest were those in which it fetched the highest prices: in the 1890s and 1930s. Those were also the times in which gum collectors were most active on the peninsula. Their lives, like those of the bushmen, were surrounded by an unwritten code of practice, and by a collection of cautionary tales — like that of the man whose rope fell to the ground after he had hauled himself into the forks of a giant tree; his skeleton was located after loggers noticed the traces of decayed rope at the foot of the trunk.

The luckier of the loggers and gum collectors — or perhaps it was simply the more prudent — made a transition from bush to farm as land became available on the peninsula. The Harsant brothers, for example, went into the forest as axemen in the early 1900s. Then they set up a store at Gumtown, which at that time had three stores, a bakery, a butcher's shop, a bootmaker, a blacksmith, a 25-bedroom hotel, two boarding houses and a billiard saloon (in the 1990s that same community, now known as Coroglen, had only a tavern, a store and a school). The Harsants took meat and groceries into the bush camps. While there they bought kauri gum from the collectors and loggers. By 1912 they had raised enough money to buy land of their own at Hahei.

The Harsants' habit of hard work was then turned to farming: they cleared trees, baked bread, made their own butter, killed their own meat and cured bacon, beef and mutton. They grew acres of oats, corn, potatoes, pumpkins and turnips. In 1920 they decided to switch from sheep farming to dairying, and bought the basis for their herd from a Colville farmer. Their produce went out by scow, which came right into the beach at Hahei, weather permitting. Their flour, sugar and tea came in the same way, or by bridle-track. After the First World War both brothers married and raised families to carry on the farming and to ensure a Harsant presence on the peninsula long after the logging and gold booms had originally drawn the family there.

Groves of kauri as high and silent as cathedrals: this one near the 309 road.

Homestead at Kennedy's Bay, an early milling settlement on the north-east coast with a violent history.

Inside the home of George, a former bushman, Kennedy's Bay.

Ossie Keenan of Tawatawa, forester and indefatigable collector of relics from the peninsula's bonanza days.

The modern forestry of pines and chainsaws is far less labour intensive than kauri milling. This man works for Carter Holt Harvey near Whangamata.

Felled pinus radiata on the slopes of Rangipo, Tairua Forest, near Whangamata. Eucalypts on the skyline.

It was timber and gum that laid the foundations for the settlements of Whitianga, Gumtown, Tairua and Port Charles. But it was gold that built Thames, Coromandel and Waihi — and Kuaotunu, Karangahake, Waikino, Waitekauri, Mackaytown and other substantial communities which have, in effect, been erased subsequently from the landscape. And it was gold that, for a time, brought thousands of new settlers to the region with dreams of wealth that seemed unimaginable to the peninsula's Maori and to the first wave of Pakeha bushmen.

After Charles Ring's discovery of gold near Driving Creek in 1852, Lieutenant-Governor Robert Henry Wynyard called a conference of the peninsula's Maori landowners at Coromandel Harbour. The result of these deliberations was permission for Pakeha miners to enter the district, subject to a payment to the owners by the provincial government. In the following year some alluvial gold was taken from river and stream beds around Coromandel Harbour, some from Colville and some from Kennedy's Bay and Port Charles. But it was small in quantity (around 300 ounces) and difficult to find. Unlike that of the geologically older South Island, Coromandel's gold was still largely trapped in quartz, which was in turn trapped in solid rock. The first Coromandel gold-rush petered out.

The second was not much more successful. Spurred on by reports of riches, Auckland prospectors returned to Coromandel from the South Island gold-fields between 1861 and 1863 and attacked the quartz veins with pick and shovel. This time some 5000 ounces of gold was extracted from the district. But then the Waikato War intervened. Many miners abandoned their diggings to volunteer for the government forces; at the same time a large number of Coromandel Maori, particularly Ngati Maru, left the area to join the defending forces of the Maori King at Rangiriri, Paterangi and Orakau.

It was immediately after the war that the development of the Coromandel gold-field began in earnest. In 1864, up behind Coromandel Harbour, on the hill overlooking Driving Creek, the first two mines — the first in the country — began extracting quartz, crushing it and separating out the gold. One of these, Scotty's Mine, was built over a scattered reef and was a financial disaster. The other,

Lieutenant-Governor Wynyard meets chiefs and tribes at Coromandel Harbour in 1852 to negotiate the opening of the Coromandel goldfield.

Kapanga, called after the Maori name for what became Coromandel township, was a huge success. Over the next 50 years it produced more than 71,000 ounces of gold.

Other mines fanned out from the burgeoning Coromandel township as prospectors made one discovery after another. The Tokotea Big Reef, at the summit of the hill dividing Coromandel from Kennedy's Bay, was sufficiently promising to attract a rush of its own in 1869. Within a year the ridge looked like an enormous rabbit warren. Only one successful mine resulted from this strike: the Tokotea itself which, by 1916, produced over 90,000 ounces of bullion.

The rush to the area that became Coromandel township was as nothing to that which occurred in Thames, however. The Thames gold-field was opened in 1867 as a consequence of negotiations between Haunaru Taipari of Ngati Maru and James Mackay, who had been responsible for buying most of the South Island for the Crown and who now became gold-fields warden and resident magistrate for the Coromandel.

Within a year there were 24 stamper batteries operating around Thames and the hills and flats were covered as far as the eye could see with prospectors' and miners' tents. Two separate settlements, Shortland to the south and Grahamstown to the north, grew rapidly to merge and form the single township of Thames. By 1870, in addition to banks, grocery stores,

Panning for gold in Coromandel rivers produced the peninsula's first strikes in the 1850s. But most of the region's precious metal turned out to be embedded in quartz and rock.

butcheries and blacksmiths' forges, Thames had an extraordinary 80 hotels and three theatres, the latter running shows almost continuously. Around 18,000 miners used the facilities of the town over the next two decades, in addition to the loggers who came down from the hills to spend their wages on liquor and women. Because money was plentiful, so was the entertainment; so was drunkenness, violence, swindling and theft.

Thames remained what it so rapidly became: the largest community on the peninsula. Its accumulation of wealth was not slow and steady, like that of Waihi to the south. It was erratic, reflecting short-term bonanzas from a series of successful claims: the Shotover, the Caledonian, the Moanataiari, the Waiotahi. One consequence of this variable record, and of the exhaustion of most claims in the early years of the twentieth century, was that the municipal authority borrowed too heavily and reduced the town to bankruptcy. For 15 years it had to be run by a commissioner.

The combined effects of logging and mining on the Coromandel landscape are apparent in this view of gold workings in the hills above Thames.

Gold was discovered in the Waihi district in the 1870s. Batteries and eventually townships grew around Waitekauri, Karangahake, Waikino, Mackaytown and of course Waihi itself. By far the most successful of these mines — and the most successful in the whole country — was the Martha which, between 1879 and 1952, produced almost 36 million ounces of gold. The next most wealthy was the

109

Mines and stamper batteries at work near Thames around 1880. The derricks were known as poppet heads and lowered the cages in which miners travelled down vertical shafts.

Workers in the Black Oak Mine take a lunch break. The firm nature of Coromandel rock meant that the tunnel walls and roofs required little support, and that there were fewer accidents on the peninsula than in South Island mines.

Talisman at Karangahake, which yielded up three and a half million ounces of bullion before it closed in 1920.

The Martha Mine also produced one of New Zealand's best known industrial disputes: the Waihi Strike of 1912. This occurred as a consequence of a disagreement between the Waihi Gold Mining Company, which wanted to put workers on competitive contracts to help stem falling profits, and the miners' union, which wanted its workers to continue to receive wages.

A change to a conservative government in the course of the dispute resulted in the imposition of a harsh policy against the strikers. More than 70 police were sent to Waihi and 45 strikers were arrested and imprisoned. It was at this time that socialist organiser Harry Holland arrived in Waihi from Australia to work with the strikers. The dispute intensified after the company reopened the mine with strike-breaking workers, and one striker, Frederick George Evans, was killed in one of several outbursts of violence that followed — the only worker to lose his life in New Zealand as a result of industrial action.

The company succeeded in imposing its contracts; a new union was formed; the strikers were, for the most part, run out of town. Seventy-five years later, in 1989, a proposal to memorialise Frederick George Evans caused so much controversy in Waihi that it had to be abandoned.

The poppet head over the massive Queen of Beauty Mine, Thames. This shaft had reached a record depth of 1000 feet by 1908.

Feelings about the strike were still held deeply and irreconcilably.

The major mines at Thames, Coromandel and Waihi were merely the most visible tip of a considerable goldberg. The whole peninsula, from Port Charles to south of Waihi, was peppered with claims running into the thousands. There were almost 1000 mines — 700 around Thames alone — that achieved some degree of success between the mid-1860s and the First World War. By the time of the outbreak of war, however, the bonanza was over. Except for that which lay beneath the Martha Mine at Waihi, all the gold which could be extracted profitably from the region had been taken — along with much bullion that had been taken unprofitably. And that situation remained unchanged until new technology and the rise in gold prices made the industry viable again in the 1980s.

The simultaneous collapse of both the mining and the logging industries on the peninsula resulted initially in depression and depopulation. Numbers dropped from 23,000 in 1901 to 17,000 in 1921. They continued to fall until the 1930s, when the population stabilised as a result of better organised farming and the beginnings of forestry and fishing. Eighty per cent of that population lived in the surviving townships: Thames (which attracted a range of manufacturing industries to add to its farm-servicing role), Waihi, Whitianga and Coromandel. The rural communities shrank. Some disappeared entirely. The

Gold workers in front of their shanty in the Coromandel hills, 1930s. The Great Depression brought a short-term revival of gold prospecting and gum collecting on the peninsula.

ranges, largely denuded now of loggers and prospectors, were left to regenerate in native bush; large areas around Whangapoua and south of Tairua were planted in exotic forest.

The dramatic population recovery came in the 1970s with the explosion of subdivisions, the expansion of towns such as Whangamata and Tairua, and the creation of whole new communities such as Pauanui, Onemana and Whangapoua. By 1993 the population of the region (including Waihi) was around 30,000. And this was swelled by a further half a million people over the summer months.

Relics of gold mining can be found the length of the peninsula in the hundreds of thousands of horizontal and vertical shafts which still perforate old claims, in piles of sterile tailings, and in the bottle dumps which lie around the sites of old mines. Many such sites are dangerous and all should be approached with caution. Examples of working stamper batteries can be seen at Driving Creek just outside of Coromandel township and at the northern end of Thames. In the Karangahake Gorge a whole walkway has been devised to allow visitors to explore a rich variety of gold-field remains.

The most spectacular reminder of the peninsula's bonanza days, however, is to be found in the working mines at Waihi and Waitekauri. These are open-cast and far less labour intensive than their nineteenth-century predecessors. Their resumption — in 1987 and 1990 respectively — was a cause of some satisfaction in Waihi, where unemployment was high, and in Thames, where pro-mining sentiment was strong. On the rest of the peninsula the prospect of a revival of mining was greeted with alarm, and opinion surveys suggested that around 70 per cent of the residential population was opposed to it. This opposition was based on a variety of factors and fears.

First, there was the fact that the peninsula is still littered with the detritus of earlier mining. Around Coromandel township there are huge humps of tailings which are bare because nothing can grow on them. Worse, many residents are mindful of the sludge left on Mount Te Aroha from the Tui Mine, which operated between 1966 and 1973. Once it was no longer economic its owners filed for

Remnants of the Luck At Last mine languish up the Wharekawa River.

bankruptcy. They left around one million cubic metres of erodible material poised on the slopes of Te Aroha, above the township; and concentrations of iron, zinc, cadmium, copper and mercury exceeding medically safe limits had made their way into the town's water supply. A mine working in the 1990s would produce in six weeks the quantity of tailings that Tui produced in six years.

Coromandel residents are also worried about the scale of modern mining and the lack of responsibility shown by the industry in past operations, and in current ones outside New Zealand (in Papua New Guinea, New Caledonia and North and South America, for example). Added to this are fears based on terrain. The Coromandel is a steep, narrow finger of land with one of the highest rates of flash-flood rainfall in the country. Tailings from old mines have already been swept down valleys and

Catherine Delahunty of Colville: anti-mining activist and former commune dweller.

deposited on farmland, coastal flats and the seabed. There is a fear that further widespread mining could endanger the now well-established industries of fishing, horticulture and tourism.

The mining industry for its part argues that planning conditions and modern technology would prevent the dire outcomes predicted by the anti-mining lobby. The groups have locked horns in local body and Planning Council hearings on a variety of prospecting and mining applications. Both have won victories: anti-mining submissions have prevented the mining of Mt Moehau, the reopening of the Tui and

116

Abandoned machinery for crushing quartz, Luck At Last Mine.

Monowai Mines, and prospecting at Waiomu; the mining industry won the necessary consents to reopen the mines at Waihi and Waitekauri.

While neither side has decisively won or lost the war, the evidence is that the enthusiasm of the mining industry is flagging. Outside of Thames and Waihi the opposition to mining has increased over a decade. It becomes more and more expensive to guide prospecting and mining proposals through the planning process, and to meet the stringent conditions laid down by the relevant authorities. The price of gold on international markets is not nearly as high in the early 1990s as it was in the early 1980s. The whole equation is not as unequivocally in favour of a resumption of mining as it seemed to be 10 years before. It now seems unlikely that there will be a widespread resumption of mining on the Coromandel; and even if there were, it is such a highly mechanised process in the late twentieth century that gold could never again provide employment and local wealth on the scale that it did in the heydays of the nineteenth century.

The reopened Martha Mine, Waihi. Minerals are now extracted from the opencast area in the foreground and tailings piped to the lake area behind.

Behind the Bright Smile Gardens stands Thames' last operational stamper battery, now working for the education of tourists.

Thames, offspring of the growth and fusion of the goldmining towns of Shortland and Grahamstown. The Waihou visible beyond.

Miner's cottage, Coromandel.

Former mine executive's house, Thames.

122

The Thames School of Mines, which once trained prospectors and potential mine staff in the science and art of gold extraction. A second and rival school operated in Coromandel township.

The Golconda Tavern in Coromandel, survivor of the proliferation of peninsula public houses that catered for an army of thirsty miners in the nineteenth century.

Early morning in Thames.

125

Helen Mason, Coromandel potter, and her mobile home parked at Driving Creek.

126

CHAPTER FOUR

A HORIZON FOR THE MIND: COROMANDEL LIFESTYLES

Just as childhood experience leaves an impact on adult behaviour, so history conditions the character and values of communities. 'Rhythms, patterns and continuities drift out of times past to mould the present and to colour the shape of things to come,' is one writer's description of the process. 'Memory, tradition and myth frame our responses.'

Nowhere do these adages have more validity and more force than on the Coromandel Peninsula. The social and cultural patterns which have developed there are a direct consequence of the region's history, particularly of its association with the bonanza years of gold and timber extraction. Contemporary attitudes — towards farming, horticulture, fishing, tourism, coastal development and environmental questions in general — are all shaped by the experience of the past 150 years.

Take, for example, the case of one community on the peninsula's south-east coast. Opoutere is a small settlement on the shore of the meandering and largely unmodified Wharekawa estuary, between Tairua and Whangamata. If Coromandel's story is an encapsulated and intensified version of nineteenth century New Zealand's, then the tale of Opoutere is a miniaturised account of that of the peninsula as a whole.

At the beginning of its association with humankind the harbour was cloaked in the pohutukawa, puriri and kohekohe forest characteristic of much of the Coromandel coast. The first known settlers were Ngati Hei of the Arawa waka, and there were at least four major kainga around the shore. One pa, Ruahiwihiwi, lay on the superbly defendable southern headland and included a deep ditch that would have effectively cut the point off from access by land. Another, on the high volcanic bluff Maungaruawahine, was one of the few in the country reinforced with stone. Deep middens around the estuary confirm that its main attraction was seafood easily caught and gathered: fish, crayfish, pipi, cockle and mussel.

Some time in the seventeenth century the Ngati Hei tangata whenua were pushed northwards by Ngati Hako, an expanding Bay of Plenty tribe. Then, in the course of the great Ngapuhi sweeps down the North Island coastline, Ngati Hako were in turn decimated and their remnants disappeared into the ranks of inland tribes. This left the district without a permanent population in the mid-nineteenth century, which enabled the Crown to acquire ownership of the land under the Wastelands Act.

By the time European settlement began in the 1870s there was only one extended Maori family living in the district, that of Tu Kaiamaire and his married children. They were joined later by Savages and McGregors, Maori-Pakeha descendants of sailors who had come ashore further up the coast. By the late nineteenth century the harbour and the village growing up on its shore were both known as Wharekawa. The first Pakeha residents were prospectors who had come over the hill from Thames and begun to stake claims around quartz outcrops in the 1870s and 1880s.

Half a dozen major gold strikes were made around Wharekawa and several resulted in mines opening in the 1890s. 'Maori Dream', 'Harp of Tara', 'Last Chance', 'Golden Hill' and 'Phoenix' were among the smaller claims worked in the hills behind the ocean beach, their names a poetic evocation of miners' hopes. 'Luck At Last', near the headwaters of the Wharekawa River, began stamping in 1895 and produced six and a half million dollars worth of gold over the next six years, making it one of the more successful mines on the peninsula. Along with 'Phoenix' it provided jobs for local residents for a decade.

At around the same time Auckland-based companies were beginning to take logs out of the surrounding hills and through the harbour. The watershed had plentiful supplies of kauri, rimu and tawa. Their value was reduced considerably by two massive fires in the district in the 1890s, apparently the result of prospectors burning off bush in their search for quartz outcrops. But timber merchants Leyland O'Brien bought the cutting rights and — to the surprise of their competitors — made a handsome profit from removing all the mature trees, many of which had been damaged only superficially by the conflagrations.

The trunks were flushed down riverbeds higher in the watershed until they reached the harbour.

There they were held in booms containing as many as 7000 logs at a time. Later they were towed in rafts to the Leyland O'Brien mill on the Waitemata Harbour, where they were converted into planks, posts, house blocks, shingles and railway sleepers.

As the bush retreated a new workforce moved in: the kauri gum diggers. Around Wharekawa they were mainly Maori and mainly descendants of the Hauraki tribes, though some came from further afield. By the early 1900s they had contributed to a community of around 50 people. The Maori among them had converted en masse to the Ringatu faith, as a consequence of proselytising by emissaries from the East Coast, and they took over a church building originally built for Anglican worship.

Down near the mouth of the harbour, on the flat below Maungaruawahine, they had a store, a bakery and a post office. Their numbers were enlarged periodically by itinerant timber workers, many of them also Maori, and by semi-vagrants still in search of gold. The government opened a native school at the settlement in 1908 with an initial enrolment of 31 students. At about this time too the name of the settlement was changed to Opoutere ('place of floating posts'). This was not only a response to the spectacle of nearby logging; it was also an attempt to distinguish the community from another Wharekawa on the western side of the Hauraki Gulf.

The sharp decline of the gum industry in the 1920s and the obliteration of the indigenous forest eventually eroded the size of Opoutere village. Residents who did not own land moved off to find work in other parts of the country or to return to home marae. The shops closed. The farming families remained; and a growing group of workers involved from the early 1930s in planting and eventually felling exotic trees in the Tairua State Forest. By the time the Second World War broke out, permanent residents were down to around a dozen families and only the reproductive capacities of the Savage and McGregor families kept the school open. The Ringatu community had dwindled and some indiscretion resulted in a tapu being placed upon the church, which was abandoned in spite of the presence of vestments, documents and collection money.

The district was now identified in guide books as a farming one. A small number of Hamilton and Auckland families took to camping there over the summer months and some eventually built harbourside baches. The prospect was appealing. The harbour was ideal for boating and fishing, the ocean beach popular for swimming and surfing. Snapper schooled off the sandspit and were easily caught; kingfish and kahawai chased mullet into the harbour and were in turn taken in holiday-makers' nets.

Plantings of pines for the Tairua State Forest began to clothe the formerly denuded hills and had the additional effect of insulating the estuary from outside scrutiny, and from the prospect of large-scale subdivision. The fact that the road between Whangamata and Tairua by-passed the harbour also helped discourage visitors on the scale that those neighbouring communities experienced. Over the next decade a holiday store and a camping ground were opened. But the number of holiday-makers remained low, even at the height of summer. Opoutere remained, in the words of one resident, 'the Coromandel's best kept secret'.

The intrusion of the world outside began in earnest in the late 1960s after the first of three small subdivisions opened the harbour shoreline to more residents and holiday-makers. This initiative also brought the district to the attention of speculators involved in subdivision on other parts of the peninsula. As the number of houses increased, so did proposals for further development. There was a suggestion that sewage from the rapidly expanding town of Whangamata be piped eight kilometres to the estuary headwaters; there was a plan for a marina behind the sheltered arm of the harbour entrance; the landowner on the southern side of the harbour toyed with the idea of dotting chalets over his headland; three groups tried to establish large motor camps, including permanent buildings, near the ocean beach; the farmer at the northern end favoured a Pauanui-type development on his property; and mining companies moved in with prospecting licences in the early 1980s.

The fact that little came of these proposals (only one motor camp had been approved by planning authorities by the early 1990s) was largely a consequence of the kind of community that had evolved at Opoutere since the 1960s. Its foundation members were Maori and Pakeha families who had farmed in the district since the nineteenth century; some were also the remnant descendants of the timber, gold-mining and gum-digging generation, now employed largely by the State forestry industry. These people remembered the plundering and the devastation that was the legacy of the late 1880s and early 1900s. They had grown up watching the landscape heal under the relatively benign effects of farming and exotic forestry. They were not inclined to allow a further round of ravaging for the benefit of absentee investors.

Most of the new residents were even more strongly committed to a conservation ethic. They had moved to the district because it was quiet and relatively recovered from the effects of the extractive industries. The harbour still looked much as it did at the time when the logging of native timber ended — better, in fact, because bush had regenerated on Maungaruawahine and in pockets and valleys in the surrounding hills. The forest birds — morepork, pigeon, tui, bellbirds, grey warblers, fantails, even kiwi — had returned. The State forest pines had softened the contours of more distant hills. The estuary itself was fringed with pohutukawa and speckled with godwits, oystercatchers and pied stilts.

Residents and visitors no longer landed the 30-pound snapper that nosed around the sandspit in the 1950s. But the harbour was still well stocked with flounder; parore, kahawai and mullet still moved in and out with the tides, and the sheltered areas beneath the mangroves acted as a breeding ground for these and other fish. The shellfish were as plentiful as ever. And the sandspit had been, since 1967, a wildlife refuge and nursery for birds such as the rare New Zealand dotterel and the variable oyster-catcher. Terns and seagulls nested on Hikunui Island just off the beach. And banded rails and fern birds lived among the mangroves and rushes of the harbour inlets.

Relics of old Wharekawa survived around the harbour, as they did around much of the peninsula — a constant reminder that the present is linked to the past. Luck at Last Mine languished in the hills like a decaying castle. One wooden boom still jutted into the Wharekawa River, a memento of the days when it had been jammed with logs. The old Ringatu church tilted precariously near the intersection with the Whangamata-Tairua road. The headlands and dunes disgorged middens and artifacts from the days of Ngati Hei and Ngati Hako hegemony. And the old native school stood as solidly as before, but now serving as a youth hostel.

These were the features that had attracted the new settlers to the district; and these were the features that the newcomers joined forces with the long-time dwellers to preserve, adopting in the process a set of values and perspectives that were shared by most Coromandel residents by the 1980s. And it has been this community of interest and this consensus among residents about what is and what is not of value to the Coromandel that has made life difficult for outsiders promoting development projects ranging from further coastal subdivision to gold mining.

Typical of the new generation of peninsula conservationists is Tony Knight, who has owned land at Opoutere since 1970 and lived there for the better part of a decade. Like many of his generation on the Coromandel he is a former radical of the sixties and seventies who has lost none of his energy or idealism, who knows his way around politics and bureaucracies, and who is an indisputably respected and respectable member of the communities in which he lives and works (he is deputy-principal at the Whangamata Area

Bee-keeping is a popular activity at Coromandel communes. This hive, suitably decorated, stands at Moehau.

School). His combination of talents, experience and designations is potent, and Knight has been the most visible and most effective member of a highly active ratepayers and residents association.

'The first fight we had here was against a proposal to site an infiltration/percolation system in the swamp at the head of the harbour, to dispose of Whangamata's sewage. We were appalled. The estuary is a base area for fish, full of shellfish, supports 25 varieties of bird, several of them endangered, yet it's very shallow. It's an easily stressed ecosystem. We were convinced that there would be run-off from the treatment system into the harbour and that all marine organisms would suffer as a result of serious pollution.'

Knight and the local residents did not simply make submissions to the Thames Coromandel District Council on their own behalf. They called in a visiting Fulbright Scholar from the University of Waikato, a Professor of Ecological Studies at Oklahoma State University who was also an expert in land disposal of waste water.

'We persuaded him to come here and look at our situation and comment without prejudice. There were no strings attached. We simply wanted an authoritative analysis. And we got it. He concluded that the proposed system was not workable on that location and that there would be rapid run-off into the harbour. Other flaws came to light: no back-up in the event of failure of the primary system, no procedure for maintenance.'

Knight and the ratepayers association then persuaded a number of experts — the Oklahoma ecologist, marine biologists, ornithologists and others — to produce a major paper called The Wharekawa Estuary Report. It outlined the state of the harbour and the likely effects of the proposed sewerage scheme. It stressed serious omissions in the council engineer's report. The document was sent to district councillors, council staff, Ministers of the Crown; anybody the association felt might influence the council's final decision. The result was a rout. The proposed scheme was abandoned, the consultants who prepared the council's original report discarded. The system eventually adopted

Whitebaiting too is a seasonal feature of Coromandel life, especially for the retired. This woman fishes the Otahu River near Whangamata.

used a variety of sewage treatment methods and sprayed the resulting effluent on to local pine forests.

The next threat was a resumption of local mining. A recovery in world gold prices and amendments to the country's Mining Act renewed interest in Coromandel gold in the early 1980s. The American-owned company Amoco was granted two prospecting licences which covered an area from Ohui Bluffs at the northern end of Opoutere Beach to Whangamata. Locals argued the case against the mining privilege before the Planning Tribunal — that it would cause environmental damage out of all proportion to alleged economic benefits and in particular would damage historic sites and recreational areas — Amoco later withdrew from its licence covering the southern part of the district.

The northern licence remained current but with few consequences. Amoco, its name changed to Cyprus Minerals, did little investigation in the district. And when its prospectors did drill, they were met by a demonstration of unhappy Opoutere residents. Local opinion was that the company and its successor were never serious about the stated intention to look for minerals there; that what they intended to mine was the Stock Market rather than Coromandel gold.

While this issue was engaging local attention an application was made to the district council for permission to build a large motor camp on land at the northern end of Opoutere Beach. 'This was a clever scheme,' Tony Knight commented, 'an attempt to develop a subdivision in the guise of a camping ground, and thus circumvent planning procedures. They wanted to create a large number of caravan sites, costing around $8000 each, on which caravans could stand all the year round. They would become, in fact, holiday homes. Every four sites would share a service unit.'

On this occasion the ratepayers association missed the planning notice in a local paper and was unable to object at the formal hearing. Several members wrote strong objections as private citizens, however. And the scheme was turned down. Within a year, a further camping ground was being mooted, this time by an Auckland lawyer who had promoted the development of Paku headland at Tairua a decade earlier. What bothered Opoutere residents, again, was the scale of the proposed development.

Whangamata on the south-east coast has grown more rapidly than any other retirement and holiday community on the peninsula. Here the township is backdropped by a forestry burn-off.

'Let's be clear,' said Knight, 'we've never opposed low-impact camping. We're all in favour of camping grounds in the traditional New Zealand style.' The new Opoutere camp proposal involved a substantial complex of cabins, which could fairly have been described as motel units, a manager's house, ablution blocks, recreational buildings, all close to an old Maori burial ground and adjacent to the wildlife refuge. 'We're talking about 35 buildings and 325 people, a virtual doubling of the peak-season population. And all this next to an environmentally sensitive area.'

When the district council approved the proposal, Opoutere residents took it to the Planning Tribunal. They won some concessions, including a more sophisticated scheme for sewage disposal and a ruling that none of the buildings be visible from the recreational reserve bordering the wildlife refuge. This decision was then appealed to the High Court, and finally to the Court of Appeal. There it was established that wildlife values are matters of national importance — a precedent that resulted in a major redirection in the scale of the development and in further environmental safeguards.

There have been other alarms: a plan to build a marina in the estuary, to accommodate boats from Whangamata and further afield; development proposals for the farm and headland on the southern side of the estuary; and an exclusive, urban-style subdivision, a kind of private Pauanui, proposed for Ohui at the northern end of Opoutere Beach. All would have had major effects on a largely unmodified natural environment and altered the character of the district.

'As far as our association is concerned,' Tony Knight noted, 'it's all part of a series of initiatives and policies which are changing the nature of the traditional New Zealand summer holiday. Once families used to go out in their vehicles with tents and caravans. They camped on private property or in low-impact camping grounds, enjoying the semi-wilderness. Then they motored on, leaving the environment basically unchanged. They may have had to endure dusty roads to get there, but they had the benefit of access to relatively unspoiled locations . . .

*Variation on the Coromandel bach: the impermanent
made semi-permanent.*

Recreational fishing is a popular pastime for Coromandel residents and holiday-makers. Many bach owners keep tractors, like this one at Tapu, for launching boats.

Holiday home, Pauanui.

141

'We have been accused of being selfish, of not wanting to admit other people to our part of the world. But we do. That's the whole point. We want other people, and our children and their children, to be able to use this area in a manner that preserves the characteristics that make it appealing and beautiful. Developments of the kind proposed for Ohui have the effect of locking the coastline into private properties and cutting out the campers and the ordinary New Zealand holiday-maker. They also mean that ultimately places like this will exist only in memories and photographs . . .

'What we're still facing is something called progress. And progress involves a group of people who move around the entire country looking for opportunities to make money from the environment. They do it either by changing its nature for tourism or by extracting natural resources. We think there are some places where one simply has to say, "No. No more. You can't come here. You've had your share."

Although outside threats have been highly influential in bonding the disparate members of Coromandel communities — and in particular bringing together the old and the new residents — it would be misleading to suggest that life there is one long battle against the proponents of development. In Opoutere, as in more than a dozen other small settlements on the peninsula, daily life is a round of fishing, gardening, bartering, tending to animals,

Angie and Ranier Hoehn, German immigrants, have established Puka Park Lodge at Pauanui: the most upmarket and most complimented tourist facility on the peninsula.

142

These Pauanui baches have been carefully designed to blend into the landscape on the pine covered sand spit.

A converted barn near Colville transformed into a shingled homestead.

walking and swimming. Some residents farm, some grow horticultural crops, some write and publish, some paint and pot, and some travel to neighbouring communities for their employment. Some are retired. There is always an influx of visitors from distant cities at weekends and holiday times.

The sense of community is strong. Neighbours are attentive at times of accident, illness and bereavement. But they also have much to share with one another in day-by-day encounters and telephone calls. An annual street party and a New Year's Eve regatta and barbecue further strengthen personal and social connections. It is as much for these kinds of human relations as for the natural attractions and the historical resonance that people have chosen to live there and holiday there. All these elements contribute to a regional culture that is distinctive and strong.

And they are apparent too on other parts of the peninsula, though the proportions and combinations of the ingredients may vary slightly from community to community. Most of the smaller settlements have developed along lines similar to Opoutere: a small base of established farming families have been extended by the immigrants of the past two decades who came to the peninsula in search of scenic beauty, a more relaxed lifestyle and cheap land. In all such places there has been some initial tension between the old and the new residents. But the stress has largely diminished as both groups forged

Cannibis high in the eastern hills: a covert but major horticultural industry.

common goals and strategies in response to planning issues and mining.

In some areas, particularly north of Coromandel township, communal living according to the counter-culture models persists — Mahana, Whareroa, Karuna Falls and Moehau survive as successful communities based on multiple ownership and a routine of subsistence farming. Wilderland, the longest established of them all, survives south of Whitianga on a prescription of healthy living, natural highs and a prohibition on all drugs. The influence of these groups extends into neighbouring settlements such as Colville and Whitianga as a consequence of their involvement in wider community activities, local body politics and social work. Many of the older residents in such places acknowledge that without this influx, their communities would have been killed by the process of rural depopulation.

Marijuana is still big business on the peninsula. Ironically, many of the hippy generation who established the market for 'Coromandel green' in the 1970s have now adopted drug-free habits in the interests of personal and community health. But some of this generation retain their association with cannabis; and a younger age group makes widespread use of it. Most of the crop is grown down the eastern side of the peninsula and much of it exported to dealers and users in the cities of the North Island, especially Auckland. In some parts of the Coromandel, this industry remains a major component

Signs at the entrance to the Wilderland Community spell out the rules.

145

of the local economy. There are others who grow the plant purely for personal use.

The most widespread local reaction to the presence of cannabis is to ignore it. But the fact that its possession and use are illegal, and the fact that periodic police raids gather in crops and growers, is an underlying source of tension in some parts of the region. And the occasional act of retaliation has made even vigilante members of the community cautious about informing on neighbours.

Another thread in the Coromandel social fabric is the large number of writers, artists and craftsfolk who have chosen to live on the peninsula. Some, such as Barry Mitcalfe, Eric Lee-Johnson, Rei Hamon, Barry Brickell and Helen Mason, have been of national importance. These and others not only ply their trade and contribute strongly to the economies of such places as Thames and Coromandel township, they are also making a contribution to community life through their involvement in the anti-mining campaign and local body planning issues. In Coromandel itself, for example, Brickell and members of his Driving Creek community have emerged as a major voice for the local conservation lobby.

The contours of Coromandel culture are less clearly defined in the towns. Whitianga, Thames and Waihi all have a degree of social stratification that is less apparent out in the rural settlements; and they have bastions of conservative opinion that have collided sometimes with the activities of the peninsula's environmentalists.

Whitianga is a relatively prosperous retirement and fishing community which some have called, tongue in cheek, a miniature Takapuna. It has taken on the character of an education centre in recent years with the establishment of a foreign language school and a polytechnic outpost. Thames survived the depression years of the late 1980s and early 1990s relatively well, thanks to local money, viable local industries and the presence of government department offices servicing the peninsula. Waihi, in spite of the revival of gold mining, has remained relatively depressed and has not yet recovered from a succession of factory closures in the 1980s.

But these places too, like Coromandel township, have been affected by the presence of the arts and

One of Barry Brickell's assistants works alongside the pottery kiln at Driving Creek.

crafts people, and of the former commune dwellers who have come to town to work in education, local government, government departments and social support agencies. That influence has been apparent in a growing support for Green candidates in politics, in the development of a more urban anti-mining lobby, and in an increased interest in environmental tourism ventures that seek to generate local income from the promotion and preservation of the peninsula's 'Heritage Trail' — its historical and natural features.

Whatever the origin of individual residents, whatever their personal values and however long they or their families have lived on the Coromandel, there is one factor above all others that binds them and stamps them with an identity: the proximity of that rugged range with its craggy tops, its steep slopes, its deep valleys; and the juxtaposition of these features with the sea. Wherever one lives on the peninsula, physical life is dominated by the presence of water and mountains. And because that presence affects so pervasively what people see and do, it becomes a factor in their emotional and spiritual life. 'The hills provide a horizon for the mind,' is how Veronica Black, a resident of Colville and Coromandel, describes what happens. Coromandel people not only have a peninsula on their doorstep; they have it imprinted on their psyche. And most feel deprived when they are out of the sight and reach of it.

Petrol pumps from another era outside the headquarters of the Colville fire brigade.

A multiplicity of options greets visitors to the Moehau community on the northern tip of the peninsula.

Catching up on local gossip at the Waihi Agricultural and Pastoral Show.

Neil Mardell: carpenter, forester, and long-time resident of Opoutere.

Farmer repairing red barn near Puriri.

Chris King, mathematician, commune dweller, alternative lifestyler: Colville.

Dan Hansen, doyen of Coromandel commune founders, at Wilderland south of Whitianga.

Punters research form at a Paeroa race meeting.

Boy Williams, a resident of Coromandel township, checks out the morning's news.

Fishing boat in Coromandel Harbour.

Fishers come in from the gulf at
Te Kawau Point on the
Port Jackson road.

Looking north from Whiritoa: characteristic Coromandel east coast.

ACKNOWLEDGEMENTS

Conversations and interviews with a wide range of Coromandel people over 25 years have been subsumed into the text of this book. Foremost among those to whom I am indebted for such contributions are:

Sarah Bell, Veronica Black, Barry Brickell, Lucy Cranwell, Te Awe Davis, Tom Debenham, Catherine Delahunty, Kate Donoghue, Mike Donoghue, Carole Fleet, Morehu Hale, Rei Hamon, Charles Harsant, Florence Harsant, Horace Harsant, Vaughan Harsant, Ossie Keenan, Tony Knight, Eric and Elizabeth Lee-Johnson, Neil Mardell, Helen Mason, Ada Mikaere, Buddy Mikaere, Jim Nicholls, Emily Paki, Norman Palmer, Te Kani Poata, Te Huhurere Tukukino, Tai Turoa, Apa Watene and Jim Watt.

I have drawn from previous books about aspects of the life or history of the Coromandel Peninsula. They are:

Begg, A C and N C, *James Cook and New Zealand*, Wellington, 1970

Bennett, Francis, *Tairua, A History of the Tairua-Hikuai-Pauanui District*, Pauanui, 1986

Black, Veronica, *The Spirit of Coromandel*, Auckland, 1985

Burstall, S W and Sale, E V, *Great Trees of New Zealand*, Wellington, 1984

Campbell, John Logan, *Poenamo*, London, 1881

Chapman, Sam, *Coromandel in the Golden Days*, Hamilton, 1975

Coromandel County Diamond Jubilee 1876–1936, Souvenir and Historical Record, Coromandel, 1937

Cory-Wright, Phyllis, *Jewel by the Sea, Memories of Tairua and the Coromandel*, Tauranga, 1988

Downey, J F, *Gold-Mines of the Hauraki District, New Zealand*, Wellington, 1935

Grainger, John, *The Amazing Thames*, Wellington, 1951

Grayland, Eugene and Valerie, *Coromandel Coast*, 1965

Halkett, John, and Sale, E V, *The World of the Kauri*, Auckland, 1986

Harsant, Florence, *They Called Me Te Maari*, Christchurch, 1979

Heinz, W F, *Bright Fine Gold*, Wellington, 1974

Kelly, Leslie G, *Tainui, The Story of Hoturoa and His Descendants*, Wellington, 1949

Kelly, William A, *Thames: The First 100 Years*, Thames, 1968

Law, Gary, 'Coromandel Peninsula and Great Barrier Island' in Pricket, N (ed), *The First Thousand Years*, Palmerston North, 1982

Lee, A L, *Whitianga*, Auckland, 1938

Mackay, Duncan, *Working the Kauri*, Auckland, 1991

Nolan, Tony, *Historic Gold Trails of the Coromandel*, Wellington, 1977

Phillips, F L, *Nga Tohu a Tainui, Landmarks of Tainui*, Otorohanga, 1989

Salmon, J H M, *A History of Goldmining in New Zealand*, Wellington, 1963

Salmond, Anne, *Two Worlds, First Meetings Between Maori and Europeans 1642–1772*, Auckland, 1991

Simpson, R A, *This is Kuaotunu*, Thames, 1971

Stone, R C J, *Young Logan Campbell*, Auckland, 1982

Story of Hahei, Hahei, (undated)

Thames Miners Guide, 1868 (facsimile reprint, Christchurch, 1975)

Waihi Borough Council Diamond Jubilee 1902–1962, Waihi, 1962

Waikato, Coromandel, King Country Region, National Resources Survey, Wellington, 1973

Williamson, Beverley M, *Whangamata — 100 Years of Change*, Paeroa, 1988

I am also grateful to the Alexander Turnbull Library, Wellington, to the Auckland Institute and Museum and to the Matakohe Kauri Museum for permission to publish historical photographs of the Coromandel Peninsula from their collections. Other black and white photographs are by Roger Hamon, Robin Morrison and the author. All the colour photographs are by Robin Morrison, whom I thank for his professionalism and friendship. These photographs are now held in the Robin Morrison Archive in the Auckland Museum Library. Some parts of the text of this book appeared in a different form in *Metro* magazine, March 1987.

BLACK AND WHITE PHOTOGRAPH CREDITS

Black and White photographs were supplied by the following institutions and individuals:

Alexander Turnbull Library, Wellington — pages 2, 5, 9, 10, 44, 45, 49, 54, 57, 58, 59, 60 (bottom), 61, 62, 86, 91, 92 (top left and right, bottom right), 107, 109, 110 (top), 111

Auckland Institute and Museum — pages 60 (top), 70, 90, 92 (bottom left), 96, 108, 110 (bottom), 112

Matakohe Kauri Museum — page 93

Michael King — pages 6, 20   Robin Morrison — page 16   Roger Hamon — page 12

INDEX